IMAGES
of America

MADISON

D1597804

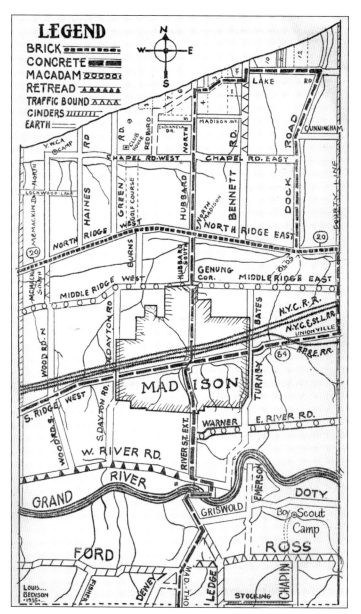

Madison commercial artist Louis Bedison created this map for the 1935 *Directory of Madison, Ohio*, published by Atlas Publishing Company in Madison, Ohio. Madison-on-the-Lake developments are numbered on the map as follows: (1) Madison Beach Estates, (2) White Sands, (3) Cumings, (4) Parkview, (5) Downing, (6) Madison Lakelands, (7) St. Johns, (8) Red Bird, (9) Madison Golf Lakelands, (10) Atwater Beach, (11) Shore Acres, and (12) Lake Breeze Park/Cleveland Avenue/Elligott. (Madison Historical Society.)

ON THE COVER: A group of four unidentified railroad workers, seated on a handcar, pose outside the Norfolk and Western freight station in Madison around 1910. Beginning in 1852, the railroad was essential for moving people and shipping products in and out of Madison. (Robert Roth.)

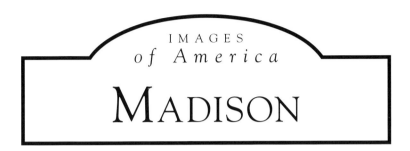

IMAGES
of America

MADISON

Denise Michaud and
the Madison Historical Society

ARCADIA
PUBLISHING

Published by Arcadia Publishing
Charleston SC, Chicago IL, Portsmouth NH, San Francisco CA

Printed in the United States of America

Library of Congress Control Number: 2009937344

For all general information contact Arcadia Publishing at:
Telephone 843-853-2070
Fax 843-853-0044
E-mail sales@arcadiapublishing.com
For customer service and orders:
Toll-Free 1-888-313-2665

Visit us on the Internet at www.arcadiapublishing.com

This book is dedicated to the people of Madison.

CONTENTS

ACKNOWLEDGMENTS

Thank you to the members of the Madison Historical Society for making this book possible. Because of their foresight, this wonderful collection of images is available as a record of Madison's past. I would especially like to thank Marje Shook for her encouragement and help with community outreach, Teresa Milanese for her expertise in editing and proofreading, and Eileen Findak of Findak Photography for assistance with the cover scan.

Special thanks also go to Nancy Hearn, J. and Fay Francis of the Madison Country Club, William Birk of the Rabbit Run Community Arts Association, and Carrie Svigel of the Madison Public Library for research help and support. Thank you to the many others who took time to share family stories and information for the production of this book, including Jeffrey Quirk, Robert Endebrock, Clare Horton, Carol Belknap, and Earl Hensel.

Gratitude goes to all the Madison Historical Society members who have contributed their family stories to help create the Madison Historical Society archives and added to the history of Madison. And finally, thank you to the historians who over the years have compiled histories of Madison, especially Gen. Abel Kimball, Harriet Taylor Upton, Violet Crandall, Mazie Titman, Louanna Billington, Viola Fritz Keairns, Mary Jeanne McRoberts, Lois Schuld, and Joseph C. Hager, Ph.D.

Unless otherwise noted, all images in this volume are from the collection of the Madison Historical Society. A sincere thank you goes to the following people who generously provided additional images to expand our story: Anita Gabor (AG); Robert Roth (RR); Brotzmans Nursery, Inc., photographs by the *Plain Dealer* (BN-PD); Cheryl Hathaway (CH); Donna Kline (DK); Beth Debevec of Debonne Vineyards (DV); Earl Hensel (EH); Lake County Historical Society (LCHS); Madison Country Club (MCC); Madison Public Library (MPL); Rabbit Run Community Arts Association (RRCAA); Marje Shook (MS); Peter Turkenburg (PT); and Bonita Weiss (BW).

Finally, I would like to thank everyone who personally encouraged and supported me through this process, most importantly my husband and family.

INTRODUCTION

Many books have been written about the history of Ohio, Lake County, and Madison. This book, however, is the first to contain such a large pictorial history of Madison. The majority of this vast collection of photographs is from the Madison Historical Society's archives. Others have been kindly loaned by residents and organizations to help preserve and honor the memory of Madison's past.

The year 2011 marks the bicentennial of Madison Township's formal creation. Yet people lived in the place called Madison long before 1811. Prehistoric Native Americans inhabited the area around Madison, as evidenced by the earthworks near the meeting of Mill Creek and the Grand River at Hogback Ridge Park (currently owned by Lake Metroparks).

In 1787, the Confederate Congress passed the Northwest Ordinance. The act created the Northwest Territory, extending from Ohio to Minnesota. From the early colonial period, the State of Connecticut had claims on the Ohio country. Most of those claims were given up with the adoption of the Northwest Ordinance, except for the area that became known as the Connecticut Western Reserve. The Western Reserve contained approximately 3.3 million acres of land. It stretched from the Western Pennsylvania border along Lake Erie to the western boundaries of Erie and Huron Counties and included what would become Madison Township.

In 1795, the State of Connecticut sold the eastern portion of the Western Reserve to a group of 35 investors called the Connecticut Land Company. A surveying party of about 50 persons, led by Moses Cleaveland, landed at the mouth of Conneaut Creek on July 4, 1796. They worked their way west and by October of that year completed the survey of the Western Reserve land east of the Cuyahoga River. The surveyors divided the area into townships 5 miles square. The land containing Madison was noted as particularly fertile and was considered to be a prime area for settlers. Madison was designated as Townships 11 and 12 in Range 6.

Most of the speculators never set foot on the land they owned, instead selling to the adventuresome people ready to settle "the West." The sale of land in Madison Township began in 1797. At that time, it was called Chapin Township. New Englanders arrived via routes running through New York state to Buffalo and along Lake Erie, or through Pennsylvania to Pittsburgh along the rivers. Many stories tell of early Madison ancestors walking or traveling by oxcart to Ohio.

Settlements cropped up near the entry points of Madison Township—at the mouth of Arcola Creek and, farther inland, at the settlement of Unionville. In June 1798, Col. Alexander Harper, William McFarland, Ezra Gregory, and their families traveled from Harpersfield, Delaware County, New York, and landed at the mouth of Cunningham Creek. Colonel Harper died that autumn. The rest of the group endured, barely surviving the harsh winter. They were led by the determination of Harper's sons, who made trips to Pennsylvania for provisions along the ice of Lake Erie.

In 1803, Ohio became the first state created from the Northwest Territory. Ohio and Madison Township continued to grow. The Connecticut Land Company appointed Abraham Tappan to set up a land sales office in Unionville. He built an office and supervised lawyers who wrote contracts for the new landowners. Unionville gained its first tavern when Spencer Shears built a cabin at the intersection of South Ridge Road and County Line Road in 1805. This log cabin would be enlarged and operated as a tavern for 200 years.

About the same time, another settlement was established west of Unionville on the South Ridge Road. Located at the center of the original Chapin Township, it was named Chapintown. When Asa Turney arrived there in 1809, there were only three houses. The South Ridge Road became the Cleveland-Buffalo stagecoach route. Chapintown was officially renamed Centerville in 1840, and in 1867 the growing community was incorporated as Madison Village. The first mayor, J. B. Hayden, was elected in 1868.

In 1811, Revolutionary War captain John Cunningham of Massachusetts purchased 2,699.5 acres in Madison Township. His land in the eastern portion of Madison stretched from Middle Ridge Road to Lake Erie. Cunningham settled at the intersection of Middle Ridge and County Line Roads. His son Cyrus settled at the corner of Dock and North Ridge Roads; son Artemas near Lake Erie at the mouth of Cunningham Creek; and son Amos on North Ridge Road near County Line Road. Amos and Cyrus Cunningham's homes were stops on the Underground Railroad for escaping slaves, providing refuge and leading to Canada-bound boats at the Madison Dock.

In 1812, surveyors cutting a road along the north ridge discovered large deposits of bog iron ore in the swampy land. In 1825, the Erie Furnace Company constructed a blast furnace near the corner of Dock and North Ridge Roads. It was later purchased by the Arcole Furnace Company, who added a second furnace in 1831. The Arcole Furnace Company was the largest industry in Ohio at that time. Between 1,000 and 1,500 tons of iron were produced each year. At the height of activity, there were 2,000 men employed at the furnace. The intersection was known as the Arcole settlement. About 200 houses dotted the area. The furnaces contributed greatly to the development of Madison. But by 1850, production was decreasing, the supply of bog iron became exhausted, and the furnaces were closed.

The settlement near the end of Dock Road at Lake Erie was called Ellensburg, or Madison Dock. Madison Dock was a busy shipping, fishing, and shipbuilding center. A pier was built out into the lake, and a crude lighthouse marked the harbor. A three-story hotel and bar, the Allen House, attracted sailors. It is estimated that about 55 houses stood along the road within a half-mile of the lake. The area also had its own school, sawmill, cider mill, gristmill, general store, and post office. About 1825, a steamboat was built entirely, engine and all, by Joseph Fuller at Madison Dock. It is reported to be the first steamboat built west of Buffalo. Other shipbuilders included Edmund and Erastus Lockwood, Harlow and Alanson Bailey, and Joel Norton. The last ship was launched from the Madison dock in 1863. Sandbars accumulated at the mouth of Arcola Creek, and attempts to enlarge the harbor were unsuccessful. By 1900, the dock had deteriorated and washed away. The settlements of Arcole and Ellensburg disappeared as well. They are Madison Township's "lost towns."

This early history brings the narrative to the point where photographs are available to tell Madison's story. This book has been divided into seven chapters that examine different aspects of Madison's development. It is hoped that these images of the past help preserve the character and grace of Madison as it enters its third century.

One

ARRIVING AND SETTLING

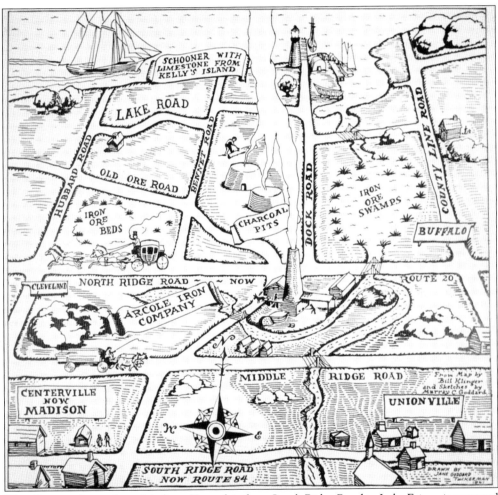

This illustrated map shows Madison Township from South Ridge Road to Lake Erie as it appeared about 1830. Note the Madison dock and lighthouse, iron ore beds along North Ridge Road, the Arcole Furnace Company, the Unionville settlement, and Centerville (which became Madison Village). It was drawn by Jane Goddard Tuckerman from a map by Bill Klinger and sketches by Murray C. Goddard. (LCHS.)

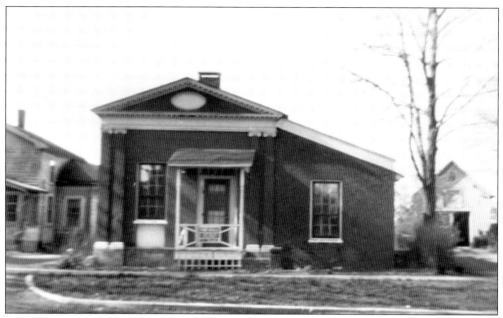

This small Federal-style building at 7071 East Main Street (Route 84) in Unionville served as a land sales office for the Connecticut Land Company. Abraham Tappan, a surveyor for the company, is attributed with building the office about 1804. Lawyers working here finalized purchases for the first settlers. This photograph was taken in 1955 prior to the building's restoration; the porch and lean-to addition were built after 1820.

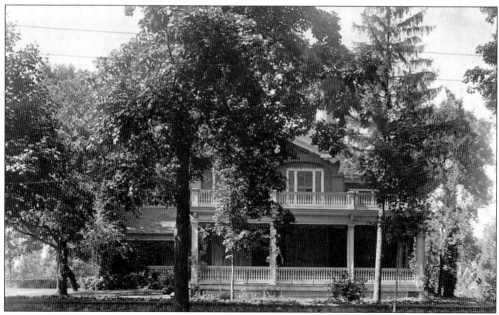

Judge Abraham Tappan built a fine home at 7855 South Ridge Road in Unionville. Besides managing the Connecticut Land Company office, Tappan was hired in 1808 to survey the Connecticut Land Company territory west of the Cuyahoga River. He also served as county sheriff, common pleas judge, Unionville's postmaster, and the first schoolteacher in the Western Reserve. He married Elizabeth Harper, the daughter of Capt. Alexander Harper.

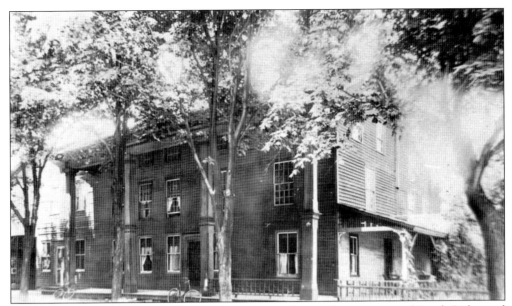

In 1798, the tavern at Unionville was a log cabin at the northwest corner of South Ridge and County Line Road. It was known as the Webster House and was operated by Spencer Shears. Later names were New England House and the Old Tavern. Successive additions brought it to the stage shown here, about 1890. During the 1850s and 1860s, the tavern was an Underground Railroad station for escaping slaves.

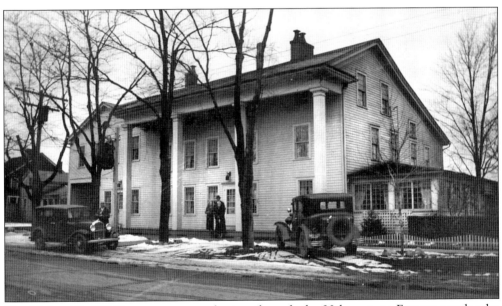

The Unionville Old Tavern was a popular inn through the 20th century. Famous people who visited the tavern included Henry Ford, Thomas Edison, Pres. James A. Garfield, A. M. Willard (painter of *The Spirit of '76*), Ambassador Myron Herrick, and Secretary of War Newton D. Baker. Here formally attired guests pose on the porch in 1932. The Old Tavern was placed on the National Register of Historic Places in 1936.

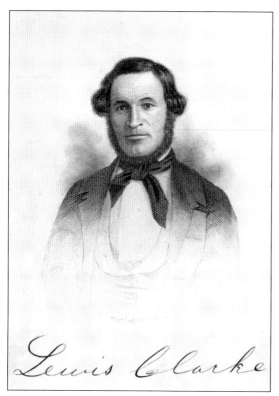

Lewis Clarke

These engravings of Lewis Clarke (left) and Milton Clarke (below) are from the book *Narratives of Lewis and Milton Clarke*, published in 1846. The brothers, of both black and white ancestry, were the subjects of a *Painesville Telegraph* newspaper story dated September 7, 1842. For the past year, they had been lecturing on slavery at Oberlin College and throughout the Western Reserve. While traveling along South Ridge Road in Madison Township, Milton's buggy was ambushed by slave catchers. A trial was heard in Centerville (Madison Village) by Judge David R. Paige. Paige decided that Clarke was the property of a Deacon Logan and should be returned to Kentucky. However, an antislavery group, led by Esquire Cunningham (who lived north of Unionville), immediately served another warrant for Clarke. After transporting Clarke to Unionville, residents and the Ashtabula County sheriff helped him escape. Milton Clarke later lived in Boston; his brother Lewis lived in Oberlin.

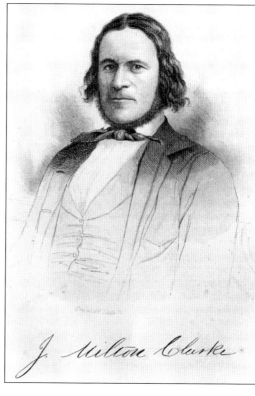

J. Milton Clarke

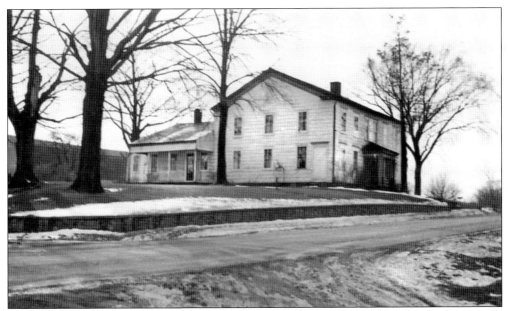

Travelers approaching the western boundary of Madison Township along South Ridge Road could stop at the Ladd Tavern. Jesse Ladd arrived in Madison about 1812 and shortly thereafter built a stagecoach tavern. A corn house on the property, Madison's first "store," was run by James Ford. The tavern house at 5466 South Ridge Road was sold to Nathan Wood in 1830. Six generations of the Wood family resided there.

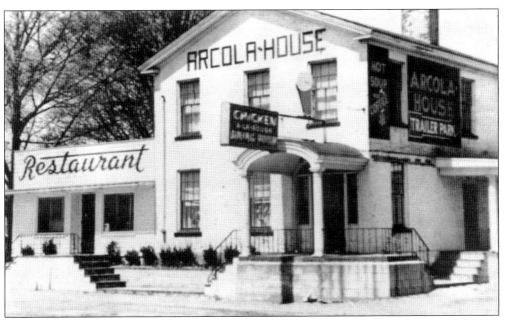

In 1816, Cyrus Cunningham built this house at the northwest corner of North Ridge and Dock Roads. Cunningham was justice of the peace and postmaster for the Arcole community. Located across the road from the Arcole Furnace Company, this busy intersection was a focus of business activity as early as 1825. In 1947, this building was the Arcola House Restaurant, owned by Frank and Mary Berus.

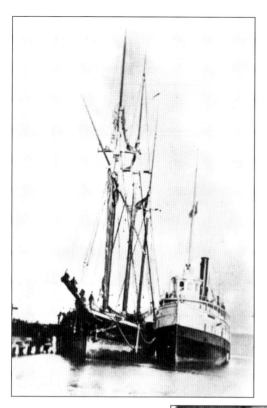

Shipbuilding at Madison Dock was one of Lake County's most important industries from 1825 to 1864. Joel Norton, Harlow and Alanson Bailey, and others built ships there. The *A. P. Nichols* was built at Madison Dock in 1861. On this vessel, Madison's Capt. Carlton Graves made what was said to be the fastest trip a sailing ship had ever made from Chicago to Buffalo—3 days and 11 hours. (MPL.)

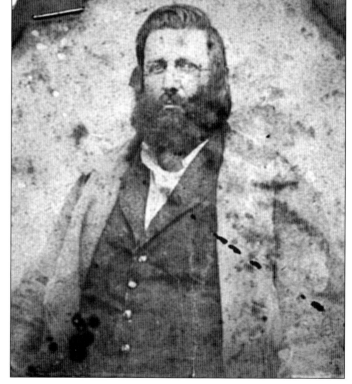

Uri Seeley (shown) and Samuel Wilkeson were partners in the Wilkeson and Seeley Company. They owned the Arcole Furnace located near Dock and North Ridge Roads. The furnace processed bog iron ore mined in Madison. In 1831, the Arcole Furnace was the largest industrial plant in Ohio. Seeley came to Ohio about 1816 and purchased land for his homestead in Painesville. (DK.)

This Ohio Historic Site plaque stands at the site of the Arcole Furnace on the southeast corner of North Ridge and Dock Roads. It reads, "In 1828 Samuel Wilkeson of Buffalo and Uri Seeley of Painesville purchased the Erie Furnace built here in 1825 and added a second furnace calling the industry Arcole Wilkeson & Seeley Co." Today no trace of the old furnace remains on the property.

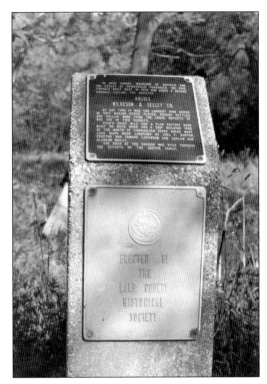

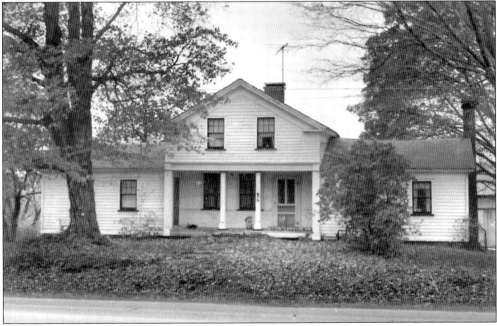

Joseph Talcott and his wife, Rebecca Warren Talcott, were among Madison's first settlers, arriving before 1809. Centerville, which would become Madison Village, was being established. By 1813, Joseph owned property at 354 River Street, across from what is now Fairview Cemetery. About 1825, he built this house. Joseph was a blacksmith and choir director. The Talcotts' son Asa was Madison's first undertaker.

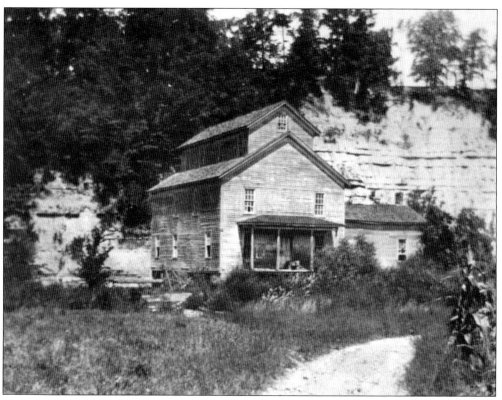

About 1830, Col. Luther Trumbull built a mill complex on the south bank of the Grand River, which became known as Trumbull's Mills. Fire destroyed the buildings in 1843, and Luther's son Aretus rebuilt the mill shown here. It was designed by John Peleg. The Trumbull Mill stood on property that is now part of Hidden Valley Park in Madison Township. The mill was torn down in 1905.

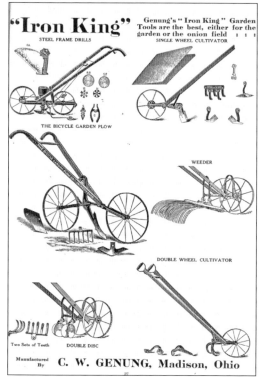

In 1842, Amos Genung established a foundry at the southeast corner of Lake Street and Middle Ridge Road. The intersection would become well known as Genung's Corners. In 1851, the foundry burned but was quickly rebuilt by William Genung. In 1867, he added a large machine shop. It manufactured engines, cider mills, and press screws. This advertisement is for Genung Iron King cultivators; several are in the Madison Historical Society collection.

Two

SETTING UP BUSINESS

Social Party.

Your Company is solicited at the

WHEELER HOUSE, MADISON,

On Thursday, March 11th, 1858,

AT SIX O'CLOCK, P. M.

MUSIC BY - - - - - - - - WEST & UPSON.

BYRON ROSE, Proprietor.

In 1849, Harrison Wheeler built a hotel at the southwest corner of River and Main Streets. He opened the 40-room hotel in 1850. Over the years, the establishment also would be known as Covells Exchange, Madison House, Temperance House, Park Hotel, and Hellriegel's Roadside Inn. This Wheeler House invitation card, dated March 11, 1858, shows Byron Rose as the proprietor.

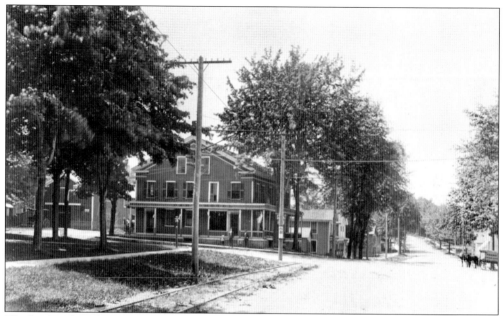

The landmark Park Hotel is shown in this 1904 photograph looking west on Main Street. Dances were held on the springboard floor in the upstairs ballroom. The interurban train tracks ran past the hotel; the stop was just opposite at the village square. On the far left are the hotel livery stables. Standing in front of the hotel are, from left to right, Wayne Snell; his father, Judd W. Snell, the Park Hotel manager; and an unidentified man.

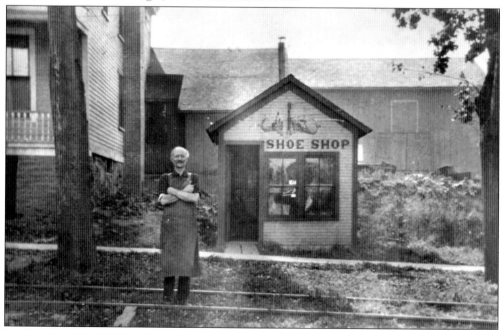

Jacob Schworm stands in front of his shoe shop on West Main Street, directly west of the Park Hotel. Schworm and his wife, Minnie Albert, came to Madison in 1897. He taught music and started bands in Fairport, Perry, Geneva, Ashtabula, Thompson, and Madison. The edge of the Park Hotel is seen on the left. Note the interurban tracks at Schworm's feet.

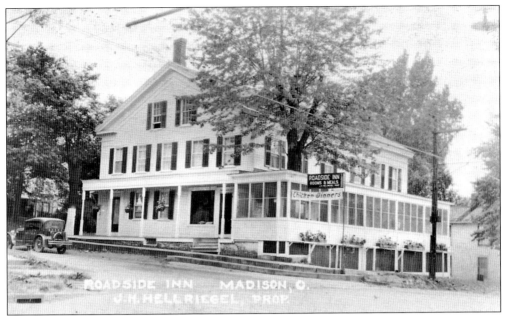

The Park Hotel was purchased by J. N. Hellriegel and renamed the Roadside Inn. Known for its chicken dinners, it remained a popular stopping place for dinner or a room. The inn was tragically destroyed by fire in 1927. Instead of rebuilding, Hellriegel relocated his restaurant to Painesville, Ohio. (RR.)

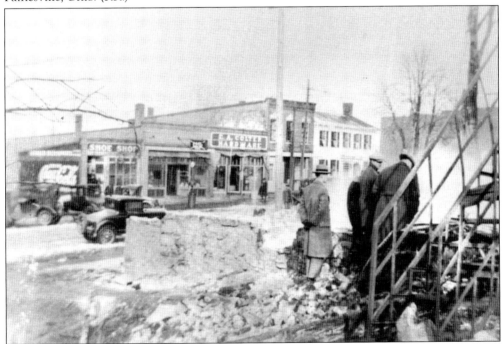

The aftermath of the 1927 Hellriegel Roadside Inn fire was a smoldering ruin. Houses to the west of the hotel were also damaged. Note the businesses across the street: a shoe shop, pool hall, and E. A. Colter Hardware. The Roadside Inn location was later used for a gas station and is now a parking lot.

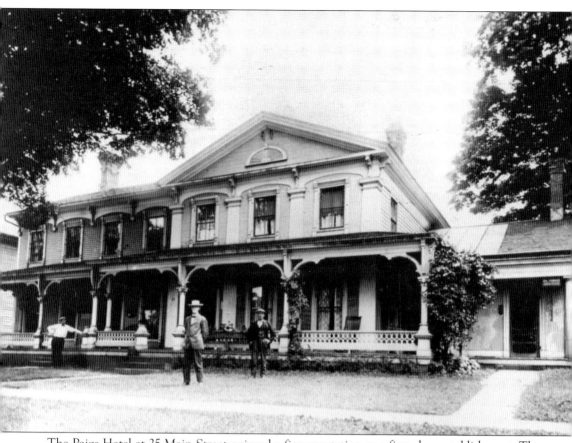

The Paige Hotel at 25 Main Street enjoyed a fine reputation as a first-class establishment. The hotel had a livery in back. It served travelers from the Nickel Plate and New York Central trains and later was a stopping place for passengers on the interurban streetcar. In the 1880s, the hotel was operated by a Mrs. Coulter and her daughter. Originally the home of Judge David R. Paige, the structure was expanded and a porch added to give it the appearance shown here around 1890. The Paige House Hotel operated until the early 1900s, when it was purchased by William and Nellie Corlett, who used it for a private residence and rented office space. This building was listed on the National Register of Historic Places in 1975 while owned by Dr. Donald Klingbeil, a Madison dentist, volunteer fireman, and village mayor.

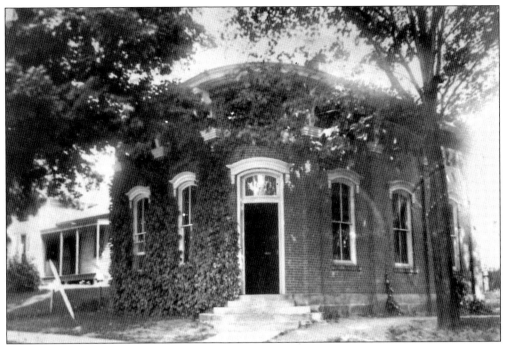

The Madison Exchange Bank, at the corner of Main and Park Streets, was established in 1875. The first officers of the bank were Asa Stratton, Lemuel Hastings Kimball, William Hendry, J. B. Hayden, James P. Smead, and director Homer Nash Kimball. The Madison Exchange Bank ceased operations in 1934. The house visible on the left is the birthplace of Frederick Burr Opper and was moved to 220 River Street in 1909.

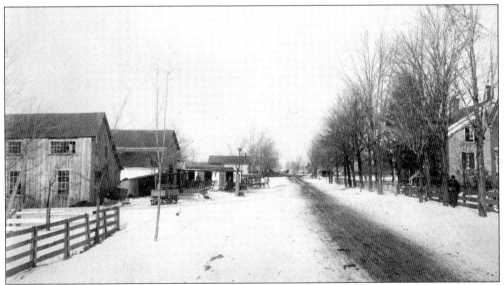

This winter view, dated 1879, is Lake Street looking north from the corner of Union Street. On the left are the H. P. Allen blacksmith shop and livery stables. The brick home on the right is the Allen home. An 1857 map of Madison lists an Abner Allen blacksmith shop at 37 Main Street. Other blacksmith shop owners were Barnes, Boothby, Bosworth, Bixby, Preston, Dodge, Copp, Callister, and Davet.

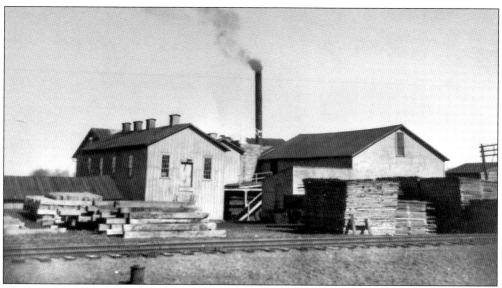

The Madison Wheel Company was incorporated in 1881. A large factory was built east of Lake Street along the north side of the railroad. It manufactured wooden-spoked wheels and supplied gears, axles, poles, shafts, bodies, tops, and cushions. It also specialized in special automobile wheels and bike, wagon, and cushion tire wheels. Advertisements state the company could manufacturer 200 sets of wheels per day. William W. Waters was foreman for 14 years, and the company was managed by Thomas Foley. This advertisement appeared in the November 1902 issue of the *Blacksmith and Wheelwright Magazine*. The company boasted, "Our prices are so uniformly low that the temptation to use an inferior article is removed." Besides advertising, the magazine ran features like time-saving tips for blacksmiths and advice for treating sick animals.

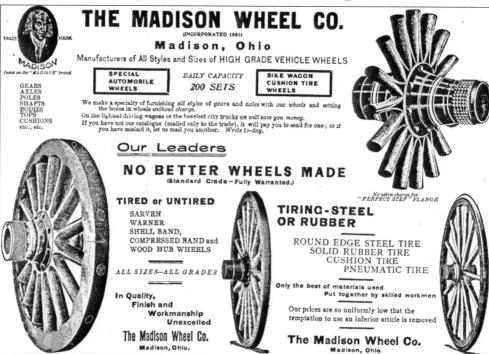

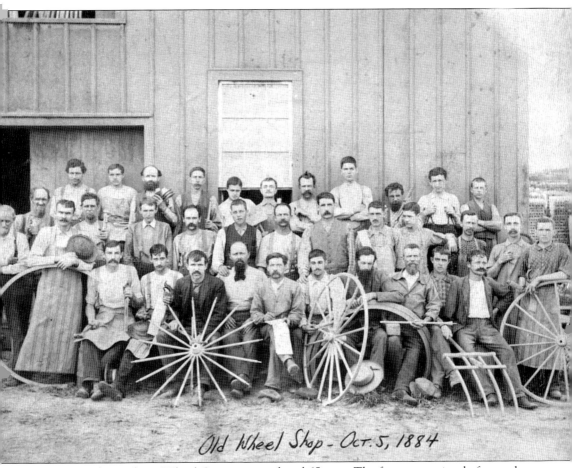

Old Wheel Shop - Oct. 5, 1884

At one time, the Madison Wheel Company employed 65 men. The factory consisted of several large frame buildings. The Madison Wheel Company ceased operations in 1914; the buildings were torn down in 1941. Many local residents had family members who worked at the wheel factory while it was in operation. The Madison Wheel Company crew gathered for a portrait on October 5, 1884. The persons as identified are (first row) Jeff Clark, Shorty Warren, Tom Foley, Del Matthews, Adolph Hettinger, ? Burdick, Olney Loveridge, Orlando Warner, and "a German who lost his arm"; (second row) ? Bliss, Mickey Molloney, ? Murphy, Chet Hasard, Jim Connell, Art Mosier, A. Preston, Charles Booth, and Clair Pancoast; (third row) Jake Heartwell, Billy Price, Dan Bowers, Fred Hauck, Art Carnahan, Dave Allen, Paul Mellon, and Shi Ludick.

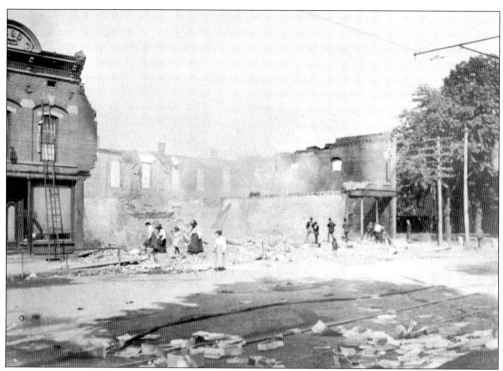

The first brick block of business buildings on Main Street was built in 1859. However, the masonry construction did not prevent several fires in the business district. The area of 26–20 West Main Street contained two stores and the "old Opera House" upstairs. In 1899, the Lake Shore Masonic Lodge purchased the property. On September 30, 1903, the Masonic Lodge building burned to the ground. The fire was stopped at the International Order of Odd Fellows building; the date on its arched facade reads 1880. The fire department pump wagon stands in the street as the fire crew and citizens inspect the damage. A horse team was used to remove wreckage. The lodge building was finally rebuilt and dedicated on February 25, 1906.

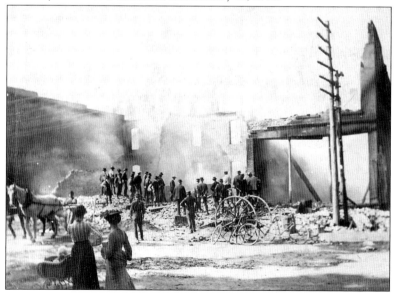

The Gill and Phelps Meat Market stood at 126 West Main Street, the location of the village hall in 2010. Pictured are Clinton Phelps (left) and Harland Gill. The buildings in this area were destroyed by fire in 1909. Newspaper reports state an overheated stovepipe started the blaze, which quickly spread to Ludick's tailor shop, the H. C. Gill Harness Shop, and Soet's pool room.

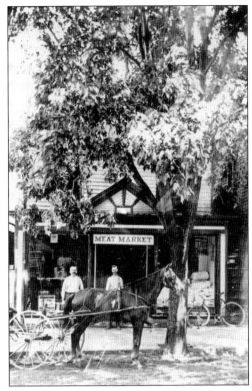

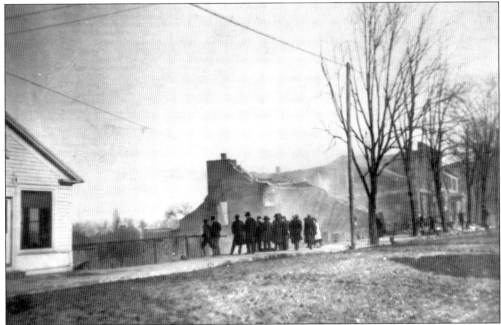

On January 26, 1909, fire leveled six businesses near the intersection of Main and River Streets. The fire broke out in Gill's Meat Market at about 3:00 a.m. Madison and Geneva firefighters worked until daylight to douse the flames. Later the space would be filled by the Madison Public Library (which would become village hall) and the Madison Press newspaper building.

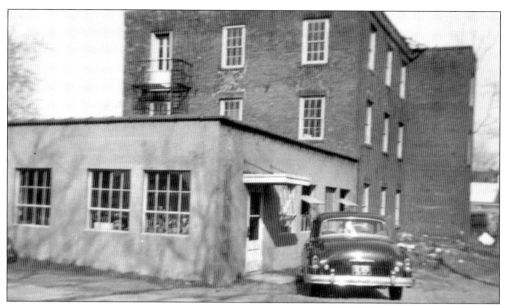

This three-story building at 16 Eagle Street was constructed about 1865. It housed several manufacturing enterprises over time, including the Madison Woolen Mills, the Roe Cheese-Vat factory, and finally Madison Basket Craft. In 1908, A. W. Teachout purchased the Madison Woolen Company building and, in partnership with his brother-in-law David Dudley Smead, established the Madison Basket Craft Company. It was later called Madison Basketcroft and Madison Willow Craft.

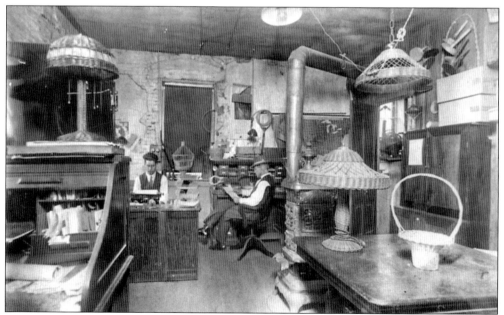

When Madison Basket Craft was incorporated, the officers were president A. W. Teachout, vice president Carl R. Kimball, and secretary-treasurer C. C. Lawson; Nelson Keyes, of Chicago, was manager. Here Teachout (right) works in the office. Examples of the company's decorative products are displayed on the desks. A 1915 directory advertised "300 different designs." At its height, the company produced 4,000 baskets a month. The company closed in 1963.

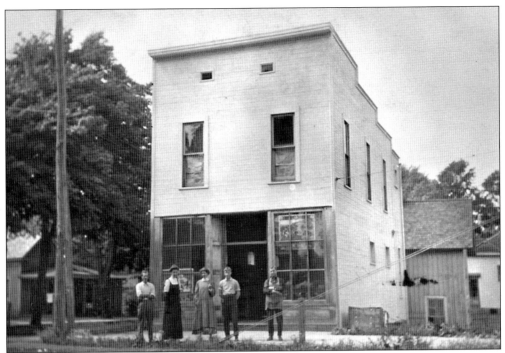

The *Madison Review* newspaper operated from 1899 to 1910. The office was located at the corner of West Main and Eagle Streets. Pictured are, from left to right, owner Vern M. Phillips, Mabel Fuller, Rhea King, Mack King, and Joe Boris (?). In the 1930s, this building was used as a service station by the Madison Garage.

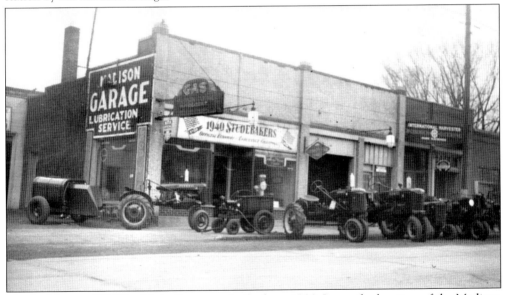

The building at 156 West Main Street was built about 1900. It was the location of the Madison Garage, purchased by Hubert P. Reigert in 1918. He sold Ford automobiles, offered the first drive-in gas station with restrooms, and had the first auto wrecker in the village. Reigert operated the business for 54 years, when he was followed by his son Hubert J. Reigert. This photograph is dated 1940.

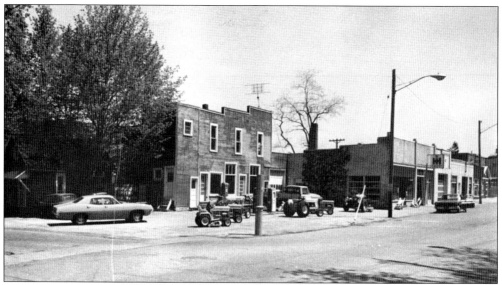

The Madison Garage sold International Harvester farm implements, tractors, and trucks. The business was also a dealer for Plymouth, DeSoto, and Studebaker automobiles. This 1970s photograph shows the old Madison Review newspaper building, which was moved and turned on the lot at the corner of West Main and Eagle Streets. It was converted into the service station area for the Madison Garage.

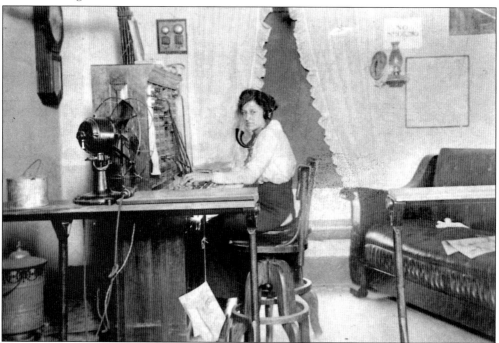

The Madison telephone exchange was located on the second floor of 70 West Main Street. The fire department bell was mounted on the roof of the building. Operators reached out the window to pull a rope to ring the bell when a fire emergency was called in. In October 1943, the dial system was installed and the exchange system ceased operations. The switchboard operator pictured here is Florence Brumagin.

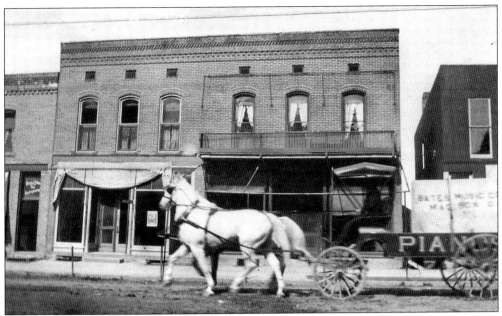

The Bates Music Company delivery wagon made piano deliveries with this fine team of white horses. The team was also used to pull the hearse for the Behm funeral home. Walter C. Behm, who was a funeral director, had purchased Bates Music in 1906. The building with the curtains, at 60 West Main Street, was the location of the Behm Furniture store. The photograph is dated around 1908.

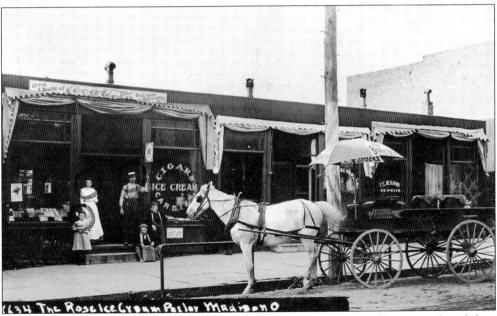

This is 50–46 West Main Street around 1910. The stores in the low building were, from left to right, Rose Ice Cream, Tonsorial Parlor, and F. E. Benjamin Jeweler, which had a large "watch" sign hanging outside the jewelry store. A little frame building farther east was Howard Wright's barbershop. Posing in front of the Rose Ice Cream Parlor are, from left to right, Hazel Rose, Lydia Rose, and Earl Rose; the two boys are an unidentified.

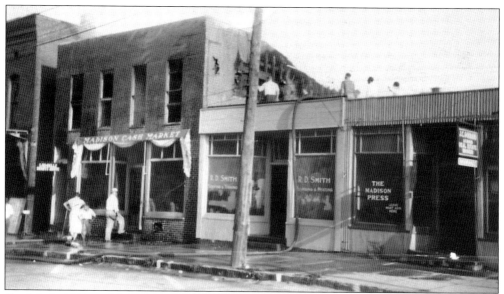

On July 3, 1933, at 56 West Main Street, the Madison Cash Market burned. Next door were the R. D. Smith Plumbing and Heating Company and the Madison Press newspaper office. On December 25, 1961, the group of buildings was again struck by fire and eventually torn down. The area occupied by the Madison Cash Market was left empty and dedicated as a park in memory of Joel Klingbeil.

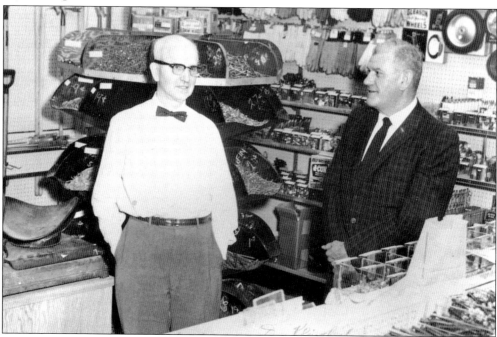

In 1900, Carl R. and Abel Kimball opened a hardware store at 38 West Main Street. In 1922, Ingalls and Johnson bought the store, renaming it I and J Hardware. One of their first employees was Madisonite Glen W. Nash. In 1947, Glen Nash (left) and Dr. Donald Klingbeil (right) took over the hardware store and renamed it Madison Hardware. In 1982, the store was purchased by David and Daniel Hearn.

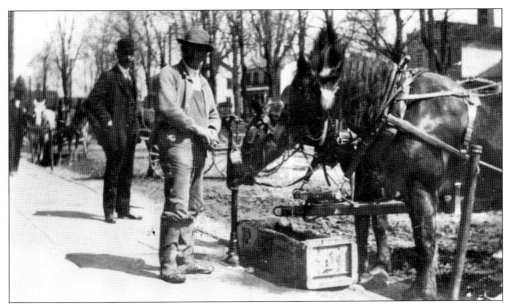

Hitching-post rails were placed in front of the shops, marking early parking spaces. Horses were cared for at a town pump and watering trough placed at the edge of the sidewalk near 20 West Main Street. This photograph was taken while Main Street was still a dirt road. In 1906, the street was paved.

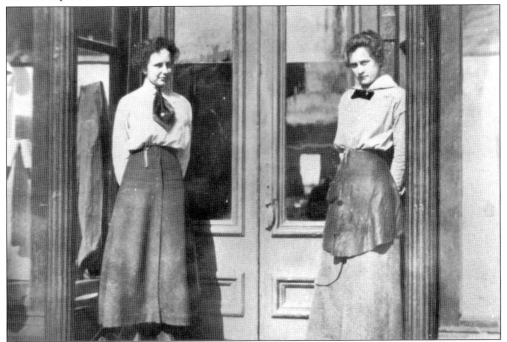

The Madison Mercantile was located at 34 West Main Street. It was owned by Fred C. Blood and later by Newton Stearns. Two employees, Julia Noyes (left) and Esther E. Graves, pose in front of the store in this 1911 photograph. In a 1917–1918 series of letters, Harriet Corlett, a later employee, described her duties: starting the furnace and sweeping the floor, waiting on customers, and arranging store window displays.

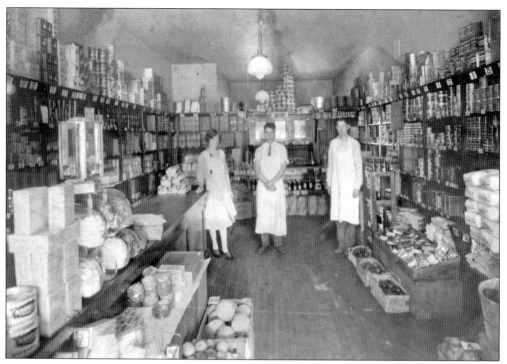

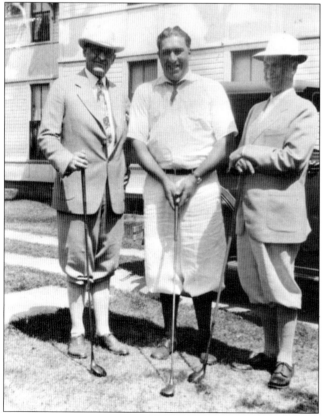

The A&P Tea Company later replaced the Madison Mercantile at 34 West Main Street. When this photograph was taken in 1927, the store was run on a clerk-service basis. Most staples came in bulk and had to be weighed. Customers could color their own oleo. Farmers were able to trade eggs and produce for groceries. Members of the staff pictured above in the store are, from left to right, Lucetta Murphy, Straley Reger, and Charles Leet. Lawrence Bayless was the first owner of the A&P on Main Street. At left, Bayless poses (center) before a round of golf with two other community leaders, Carl R. Kimball (left) and James P. Smead.

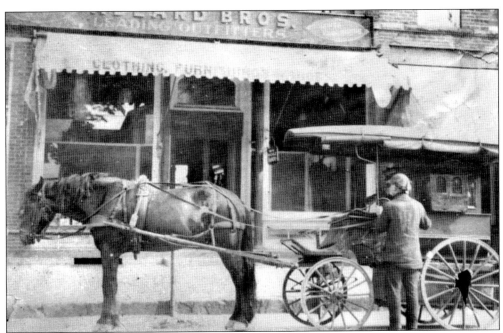

Adlard Brothers Leading Outfitters was located at 30 West Main Street on the lower level of the International Order of Odd Fellows building. It was operated by Will and Walter Adlard. The store sold men's shirts, hats, wool suits, and coats and advertised "spring arch shoes." In later years, clothing shops along Main Street included the Mary Evelyn Shop and Jerry-Faye's House of Family Wear.

In 1923, Fred C. Ellis Sr., shown here, partnered with John Ritola to form the Paragon Pharmacy at 26 West Main Street. In 1943, Ellis purchased Ritola's share and renamed the store Ellis Pharmacy. He operated the drugstore until he retired in 1963. Ellis was well known for his portrayal of Santa Claus at the annual Christmas in the Village Park event.

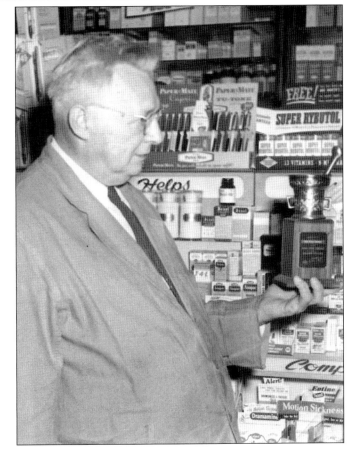

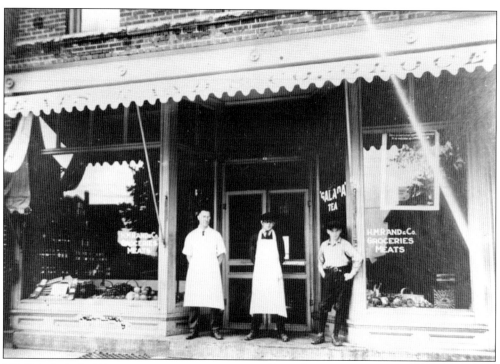

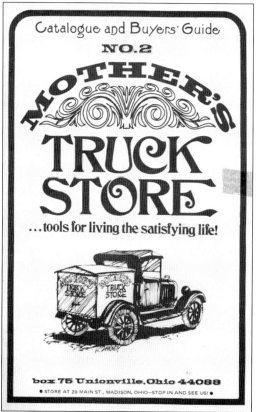

Catalogue and Buyers' Guide

NO.2

MOTHER'S

TRUCK STORE

...tools for living the satisfying life!

box 75 Unionville, Ohio 44088

● STORE AT 20 MAIN ST., MADISON, OHIO—STOP IN AND SEE US! ●

Several grocery stores appeared along Main Street. H. M. Rand and Company was owned by Harry and Arthur Rand. The meat market and grocery store was located at 20 West Main Street. Pictured above from left to right are Murray Goddard (Harry Rand's son-in-law), Arnold Radke, and Raymond Harper. In 1971, the building at 20 West Main Street was occupied by Mother's Truck Store, which sold old-time tools and ecologically conscious products to "modern homesteaders." The store and mail-order catalog (at left) was the sales division of the *Mother Earth News* magazine. The magazine, started in 1970 by John and Jane Shuttleworth of Madison, focused on the back-to-the-land movement of the 1970s.

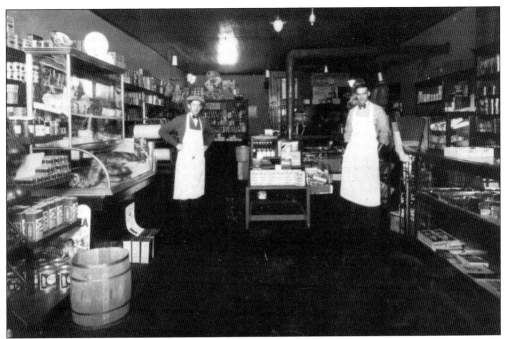

The Madison Grocery Company was located at 16–18 Main Street. The store was managed by E. G. Smith. An advertisement in the 1935 *Directory of Madison, Ohio* listed a variety of household items, school supplies, and toys, as well as food, in their well-stocked inventory. Charles McLean (right) is pictured in the store's interior.

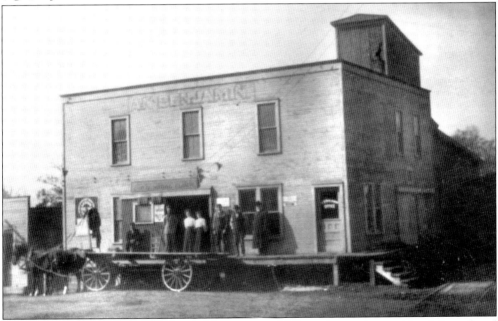

Alan N. Benjamin established the A. N. Benjamin Mill on the southwest side of the railroad crossing on Lake Street. The building served as a major hub for supplying farmers and shipping their produce by rail. This 1910 photograph shows the Benjamin name painted at the top of the building. Benjamin and his staff pose on the loading dock with their delivery wagon.

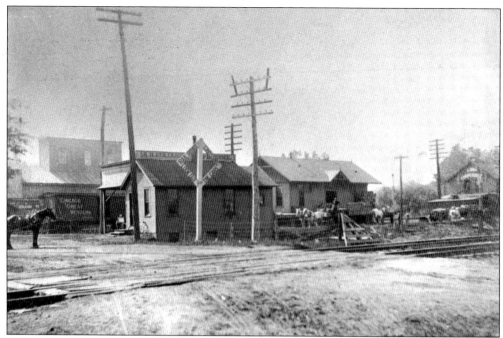

The railroad crossing was a bustle of activity. This view is looking southwest across the railroad tracks. The A. N. Benjamin Mill is visible at the far left. The small building at the center of the photograph is the A. N. Benjamin Produce depot for shipping produce. A wagon team delivers onions to the station building in the center right. On the far right, the Lucian Gale Cooperage manufactured barrels for packing produce.

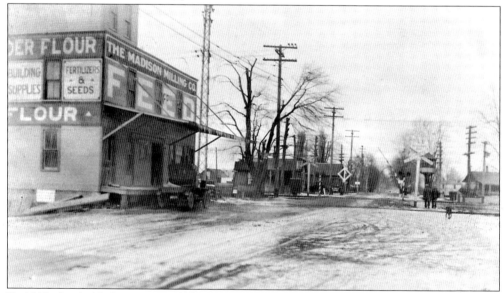

By 1915, the A. N. Benjamin Mill had become the Madison Milling Company. In this 1920s photograph, the Madison Milling Company had added more signs but retained the loading dock and overhang facing Lake Street. Looking north on Lake Street, the old A. N. Benjamin Produce depot building is still visible. A tall electrical tower has been built near the railroad, and a safety gate has been added to the crossing.

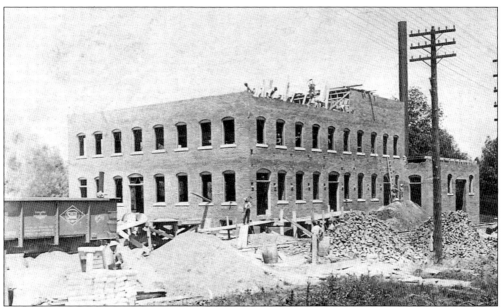

In 1914, the William Edwards Canning Company was constructed on Edwards Street just north of the New York Central railroad tracks. William Edwards owned a large farm on Chapel Road east of the Madison Country Club. The farm extended to the banks of Lake Erie. Tomatoes were the main crop. The new factory weighed produce by the wagonload and used automated conveyors to speed production of ketchup, chili sauce, and sauerkraut. The Edwards Canning Company operated from 1914 to 1934. In 1934, Sunset Wines, Inc. set up business in the building. Lorito Lazarony was the manager and winemaker there. Other companies to use the building were Floyd A. Holes Company (1950s), Leeco Corporation (1957–1983), and Acme Resin (1983–1987). The building was demolished in January 2000.

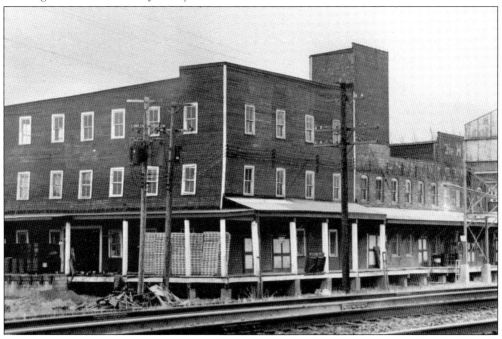

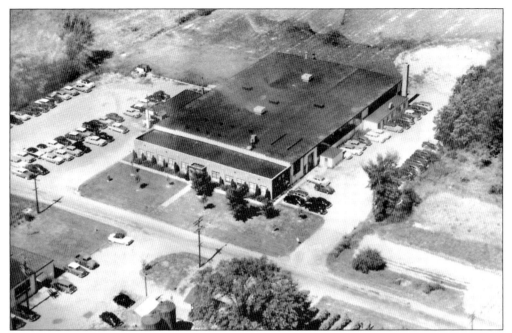

The Euclid Electric Company built a new plant in Madison on Edwards Street in 1947. In 1966, it was purchased by the Harvey Hubbell Company. The company produced industrial controls and switches for a wide range of applications, including machine tools, trucks, and conveyors. It employed about 150 people. The building was taken down in 2009.

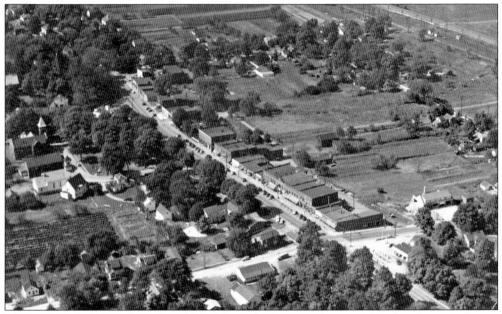

This view of Madison Village was taken in the early 1970s. By this time, a modern business district had grown up along North Ridge Road, creating competition for the owners of village businesses. However, the historic flavor of the original Madison business district continues to draw creative proprietors. The village square and the buildings on Main Street have been designated a National Register Historic District by the Ohio Historical Society.

Three
VILLAGE HOMES
AND FAMILIES

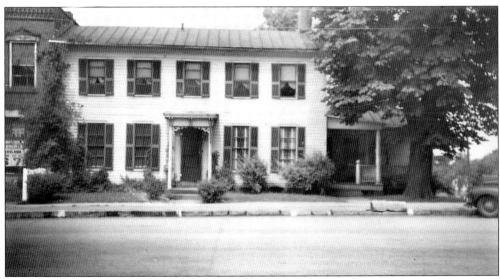

Elisha Wood came to Ohio in 1817 and settled in Madison in 1823. In 1825, he married Polly Doty. He purchased an existing tannery and built this home on 100 West Main Street in 1827. The strategic location at the crossroads leading south on the Thompson Road (now River Street) was perfect for the growing enterprise. The house was occupied by the extended Wood family for 115 years.

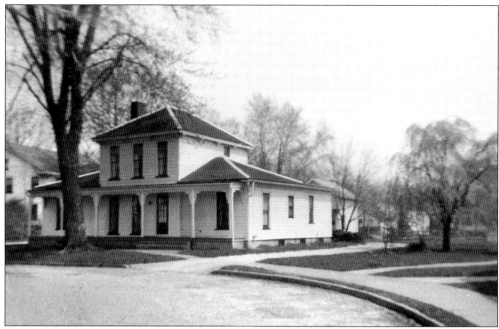

John Kellogg came to Madison in 1823 at age 23, traveling by foot from Massachusetts. He opened a blacksmith shop and later purchased property in the village. The land at 25 Park Street on the east side of the village square was originally owned by Kellogg. He passed it on to his children. His daughter Mary and her husband, Nathaniel Holbrook, built this house in 1861.

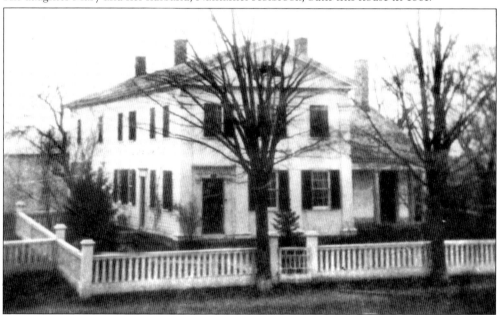

David R. Paige was born in Rutland, Vermont, in 1806 and arrived in Madison in 1832. He set up a business as a merchant. In 1835, he built this Federal-style house at 25 Main Street in Madison Village. It was designed and constructed by his future brother-in-law Addison Kimball. In 1863, David and Nancy Paige moved to Painesville. Their home would become the Paige House Hotel.

David R. Paige was an influential member of the community. He was appointed to serve among the first group of associate judges of the Lake County court of common pleas, between 1840 and 1846. David was an original director and contributed funds to the establishment of the interurban Cleveland, Painesville, and Ashtabula Railroad. He originated the Painesville Savings and Loan and served as its director. He was also a trustee for the Lake Erie Seminary, which later became Lake Erie College. Nancy Kimball Paige was the daughter of Lemuel Kimball and Polly Cutler. She came with her parents to Madison in 1812 from Rindge, New Hampshire. Nancy married David Paige in 1837. They had seven children.

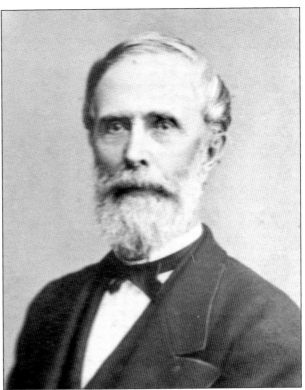

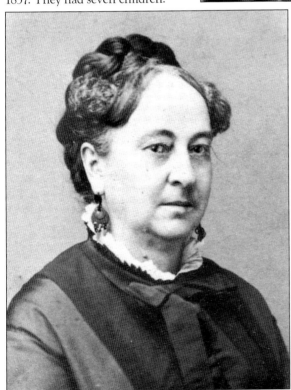

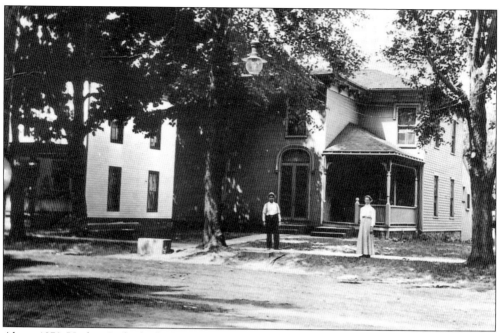

About 1870, Harlow Bailey built this house at 38 River Street. Harlow was the owner and operator of the Bailey shipyards on Dock Road. Pictured in front of the house are Charles and Jenny Ford, later owners of the home. The house was subsequently purchased by the Behm family and became part of the Behm funeral home complex.

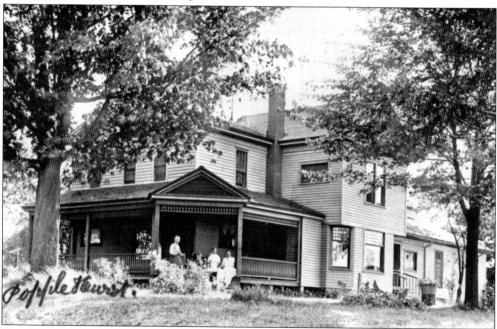

This large home owned by Sidney and Nellie Tompkins stood at 560 River Street. Sitting on the porch around 1908 from left to right are Halina Scott, Evelyn Tompkins, and Evelyn's mother, Nellie Pierce Tompkins. The house was later known as the Burt-Abby home. It was demolished in 1964 when the Interstate 90 interchange was constructed, and a gas station was built on the site.

Dr. Jotham C. Winans came to Madison in 1868 and set up a medical practice. Seen here in 1879, Dr. Winans and his wife, Julia Bortner Winans, pose for the camera. Their home was the ornate Victorian house with Eastlake-style trim at 143 River Street. According to Madison tradition, the older rear portion of the structure was built by Lemuel Kimball on his West Main Street homestead and moved to the River Street location.

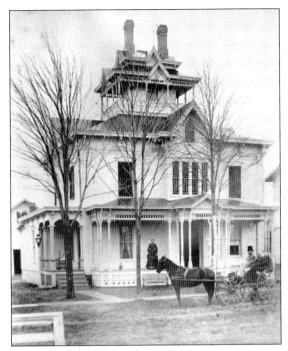

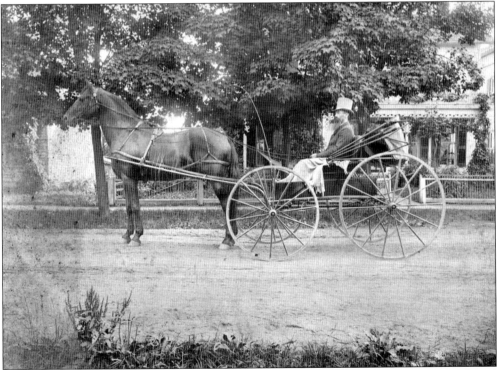

Dr. Jotham C. Winans is the country doctor in this fine buggy. His son, Dr. J. Vern Winans, followed his father in the medical profession, served as a state legislator, and led in the establishment of the Lake County Health Department. Dr. J. Vern Winans was instrumental in the establishment of the first telephone line to serve Madison in 1896. His phone number was "3."

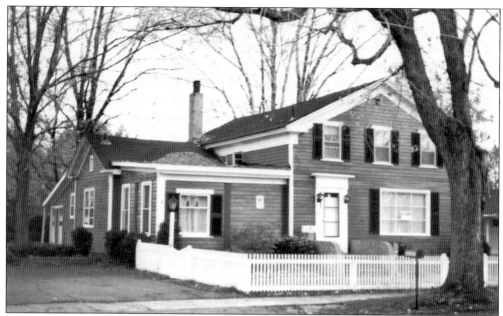

About 1842, Charles and Polly Burr built their home on Main Street east of the Madison Exchange Bank. In 1909, the house was moved to 220 River Street, where it stands today. Charles Burr was a cooper and supplied barrels to, among others, local still owners. The Burrs raised 10 children here. Their daughter Aurelia married Lewis Opper; their son Frederick Burr Opper was born in Madison in 1857.

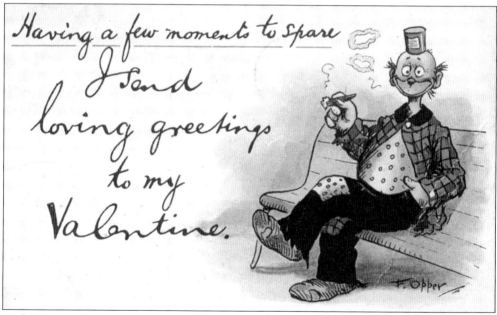

Frederick Burr Opper was famous for his cartoon character Happy Hooligan, shown here on a Valentine card printed in 1904. Opper left school at age 14 and worked in a Madison general store, then the village newspaper, where he learned the print trade. He went to New York City at age 16, where his career as a cartoonist began. His characters appeared in newspapers, books, cartoons, and live-action movie shorts.

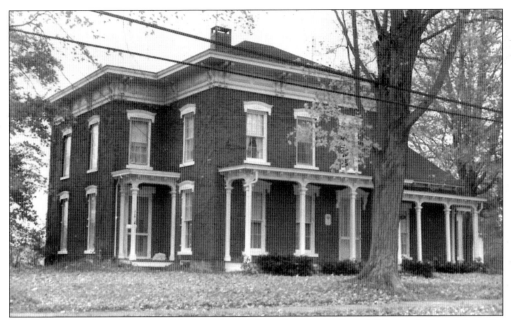

In 1848, David Smead came to Madison from Massachusetts and established a 120-acre farm. In 1863, he hired Robertus Childs to build this house at 269 East Main Street. Smead's son James Porter was a legislator and principal stockholder of the Exchange Bank; son Samuel was a surgeon; daughter Sarah was a teacher. Grandson David Dudley Smead was a partner in Madison Basket Craft and mayor of Madison Village.

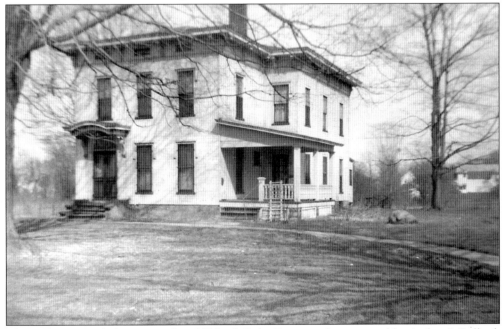

This Italianate-style home stood at 46 North Lake Street and was owned by Arthur J. Bollard. Bollard was the original owner of the *Madison Review* newspaper, partnering with Homer Nash Kimball. The house sat back from the road with a large curved walkway. This photograph was taken in 1957. The house was removed for a commercial building in the 1960s.

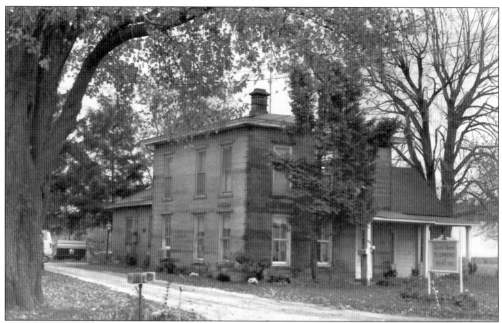

This house at 298 Lake Street was built by John Jones about 1874 as his family home. The house is unusual in that it was constructed from sandstone that was hauled from Thompson. The stone blocks in the house are 16 inches thick and vary in length up to 5 feet. Jones was a stonemason born in England who arrived in Madison sometime before 1870.

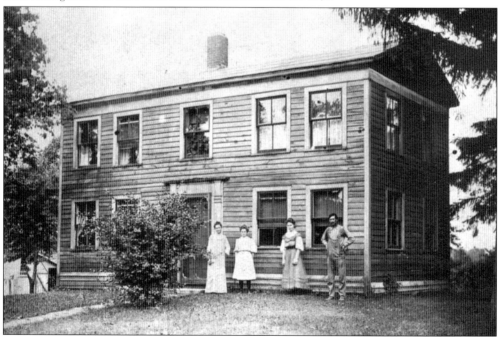

John R. Graves built this home at 6738 Middle Ridge Road at the intersection of Genung Road. John worked at William Genung's Iron King Company across the street. In this c. 1906 photograph are, from left to right, Lottie, Esther, Alta, and John R. Graves. The barn on the farm is gone; the house still stands, although somewhat altered.

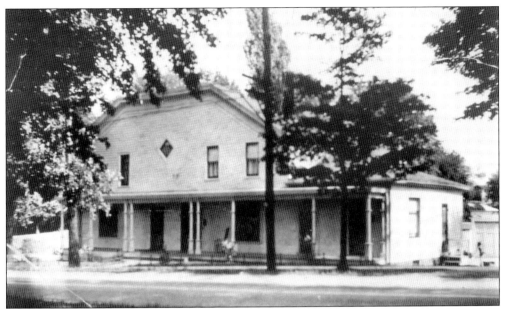

The unusual house at 189–195 West Main Street is actually two houses combined. This 1920 photograph shows the house shortly after completion. Jane Gilbert hired Madison contractor Herbert Swaby to connect the houses and convert them into a boardinghouse. Originally the east part of the house was a coffin factory. The west part, originally built about 1839, was later used as doctors' offices by Dr. Vine Hall Tuttle and Dr. Good.

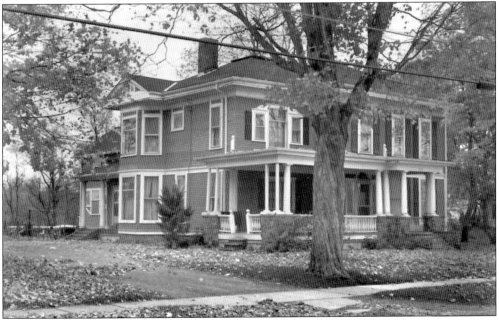

About 1870, Alpha Childs, son of master builder Robertus Childs, built this home at 319 West Main Street. The house features stained glass, Palladian windows, oak and cherry paneling, and a two-story carriage house. In 1910, the house was owned by Dr. Charles H. Quayle, who used it as a tuberculosis sanitarium. A later directory advertisement promoted the sanitarium as "a retreat for Drug Addicts, Alcoholics, and Neuesthenics [sic]."

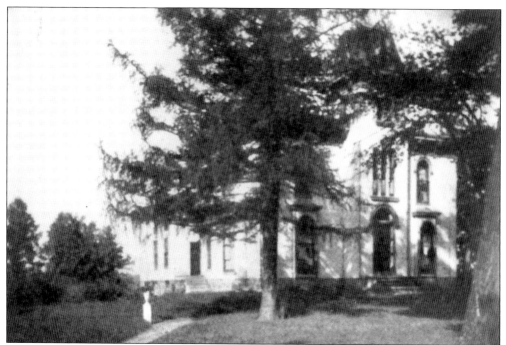

This house at 790 West Main Street was known as Evergreen Home. It was built in 1860 by Horace Ensign. His daughter Frances married William E. Fuller. William and Frances then lived in the home. Frances was a well-known national organizer and lecturer for the Women's Christian Temperance Union. She was president and served in the organization for over 40 years.

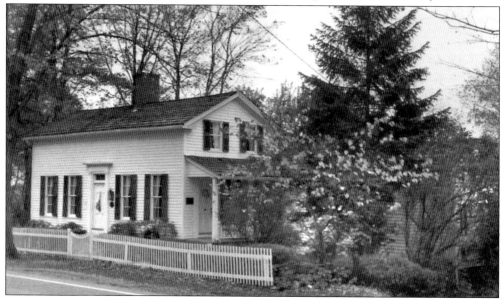

The home of Addison Kimball and his wife, Samantha Webster, at 390 West Main Street, was built in 1825. It was occupied by the extended Kimball family until 1958. The practical yet beautiful Federal design of the house is similar to several others in the village that were built by Addison Kimball. This photograph was taken in 1979 when the house was listed on the National Register of Historic Places.

Addison Kimball was born in Rindge, New Hampshire, and was the son of Lemuel Kimball. The Kimballs arrived in Madison in 1812 when Addison was six years old. Trained as a carpenter, Addison built many of the homes in Madison. He also was employed by the Lake Shore Railroad and superintended the building of all the depots and roundhouses on the line from Cleveland to Erie.

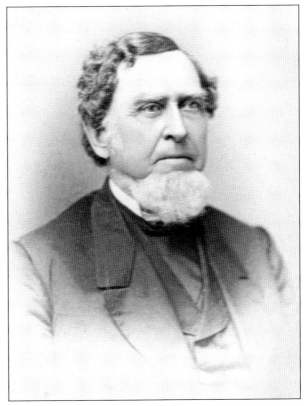

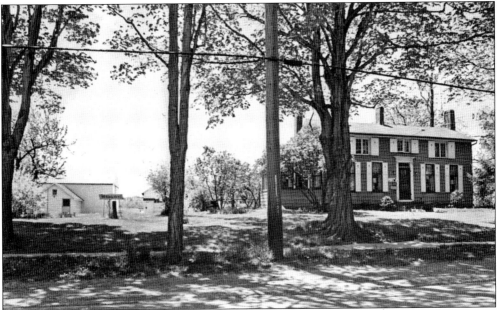

The house at 391 West Main Street belonged to Solomon Cutler Kimball and his wife, Sara Wright. Solomon was born in 1794, the first child of Lemuel Kimball and Polly Cutler Kimball. The house was built in 1825. It sits on a portion of the original 1,000 acres purchased by brothers Lemuel and Abel Kimball.

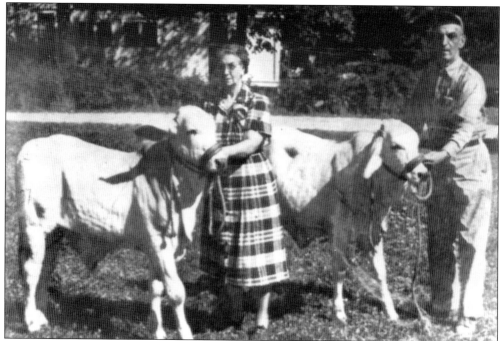

Beginning in 1935, the old Solomon Cutler Kimball property was the home of John (right) and Alma Ritola (left). They named the home Old Colony Farm. John instituted modern methods on his village farm, including the invention of the "Driv-Thru electrically charged gate." John and Alma Ritola owned many other business enterprises in Madison, including the Bluebird Café, the Lake Store, and the Paragon Drug Store.

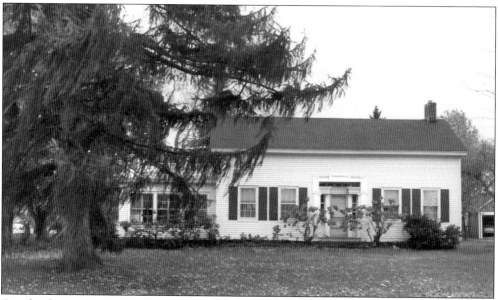

Another home designed and built about 1840 by Addison Kimball sits at 939 West Main Street. It was owned by James Dayton, a cattle dealer and shipper. Dayton purchased cattle from Texas and had them shipped via railroad to his farm located near the railroad line. Cattle were herded up the hill from the railroad, butchered at the farm, and then sent on to Buffalo.

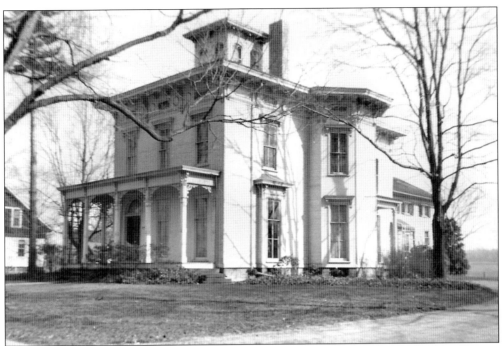

The son of Abel Kimball II, Lemuel Hastings Kimball, was born in Madison in 1833. Following the Civil War, he replaced the older family home with this stately home at 467 West Main Street. In 1868, he moved the old house to 143 River Street, cleared virgin timber from his land, and built what was considered one of the finest homes in Madison. Construction of the house took two years.

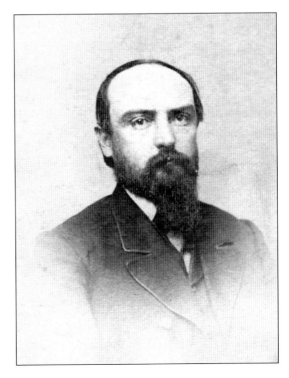

Lemuel Hastings Kimball, shown here, married Caroline Nash in 1866. Their five children all attended Oberlin College. Homer became superintendent of Madison Schools and served in the Ohio Legislature. Abel was Lake County treasurer for 12 years. Helen and Elizabeth worked at the Madison Exchange Bank, and later Elizabeth worked at the county treasurer's office. Carl served three terms at the Ohio Legislature, the last as speaker.

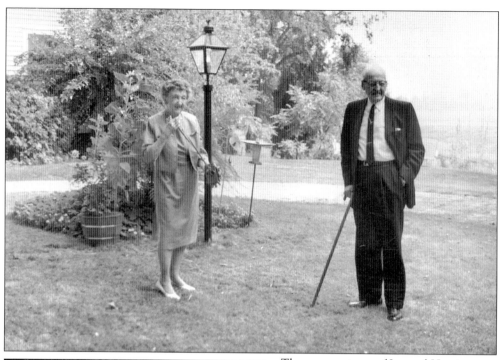

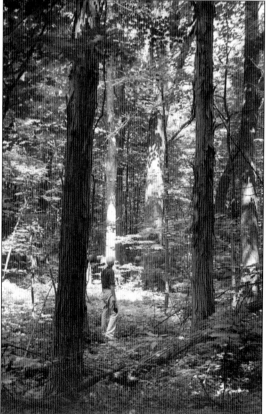

The youngest son of Lemuel Hastings Kimball and Caroline Kimball, Carl R. Kimball, married Ethel Sutton in 1903. Carl and his brother Abel formed the Kimball Brothers Hardware. Carl was elected to the Ohio State Legislature and was treasurer of Andrews School in Willoughby. Ethel Kimball was a member of the faculty there, teaching organ and piano. Here the Kimballs enjoy the garden at the family home at 467 West Main Street.

In 1962, Carl and Ethel Kimball donated 57 acres of undeveloped woodlands to the Nature Conservancy so that it would be preserved and studied in its natural state. The property was named Kimball Woods, with Kent State University named as the property custodian. The 57 acres were part of the original 1,000 acres purchased by Lemuel and Abel Kimball from the Connecticut Land Company in 1812.

Four

BUILDING A COMMUNITY

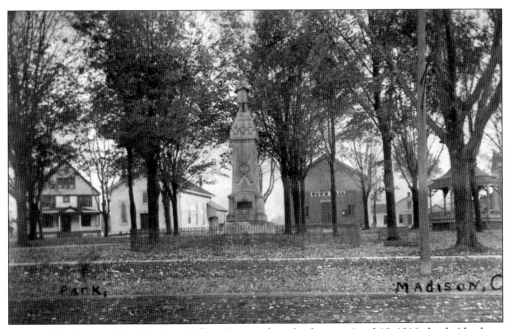

The establishment of the Madison Village Square dates back to an April 19, 1816, deed. Abraham and Elizabeth Tappan sold "three acres and one quarter of land" situated "on the ridge road" to a group of Madison trustees. The selling price was $32.64. The land was designated for public and religious meeting houses and, at the east side, a burying ground.

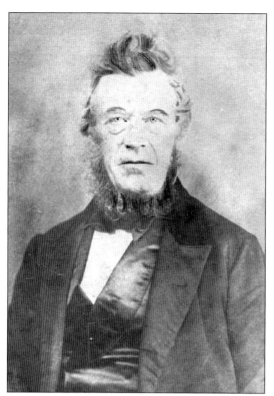

Martin Rand was born in Harvard, Massachusetts, in 1801. In 1824, he married Lucy Cummings. The next year, they came to Madison and settled on Middle Ridge Road. Rand was one of the original trustees of Madison; his name appears among those carved over the door of the old town hall on the village square. Lucy Cummings Rand was born in Brookline, New Hampshire, in 1805. The Rands raised their children, Elmer, Silas, and Henry C., on their Middle Ridge farm. They all remained in Madison.

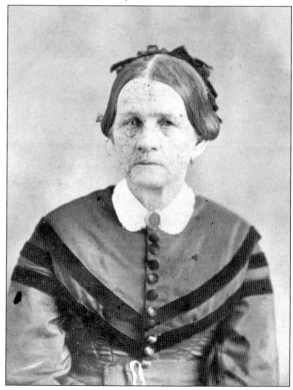

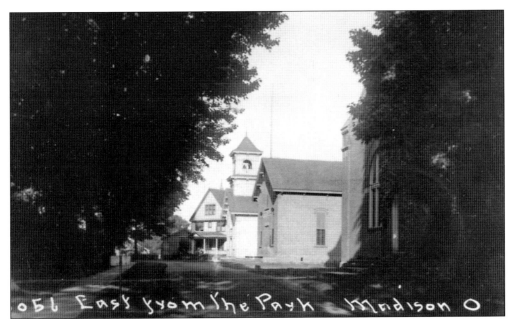

In 1828, a church was built on the south side of the village square at 49 Park Street. In 1842, the building was turned over to township officials for use as a town hall. In 1867, the building was expanded. Trustees Eli Olds, Martin Rand, and E. B. Griswold are credited in stone over the doorway. The building contractors were Pancost and Turber. This photograph was taken in 1915.

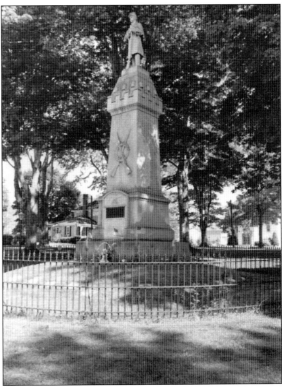

On July 5, 1897, Madison dedicated this monument on the village square "in memory of the soldiers and sailors who gave their lives in defense of their country 1861–1865." Stones honoring men from the following families circle the monument: Fuller, Griswold, Thompson, Parsons, Harris, Olds, Allen, Multer, Benton, Bliss, Nash, Mosier, Rosa, Kellogg, St. John, Daniels, Lee, C. Barber, B. Barber, Woodworth, Foster, Truax, Randall, Whiting, and Wright.

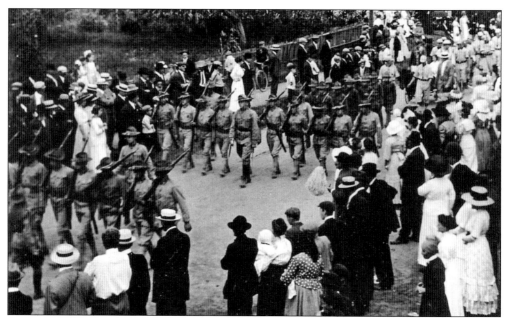

On August 15, 1912, Unionville held a Home Coming and Industrial Fair. The event was chaired by Katherine Warner. A grand concert was organized by Frederic M. Nicholas and Charles H. Hopper. The 1912 parade at Unionville was an ornate affair with historical floats, carriages, and military groups. Uniformed troops marched along County Line Road past the appreciative crowd.

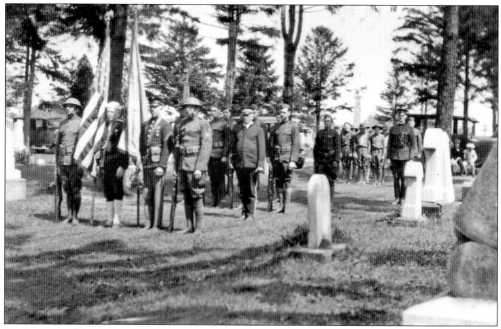

Madison World War I veterans participated at this Memorial Day cemetery observation in the 1920s. Nicholas Emmel (second from left, holding the American flag) served in the U.S. Navy from 1917 to 1919. Following the war, he owned a bakery at 1 Main Street. Also in the photograph are Capt. Donald Wheeler, Stanley Bates, Howard Wright, ? Van Dyke, and Dr. Vern Winans.

Time passed and America endured World War II. Ceremonies honoring Madison's veterans continued on the village square. This photograph taken in the early 1950s shows a veteran being honored under the original park gazebo. The Madison High School Band and attentive children listen to the program. Similar observations are still repeated every year in Madison. The wood gazebo was taken down in 1955 and replaced with a brick pavilion.

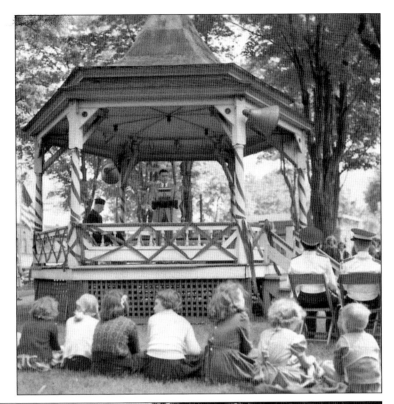

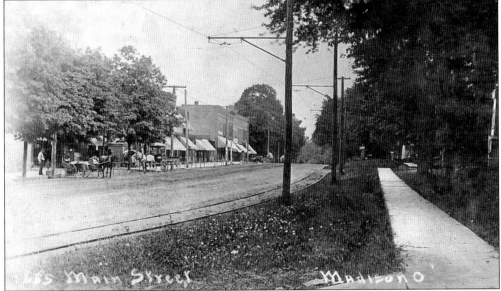

In 1895, the Cleveland, Painesville, and Eastern Railroad Company was founded. The interurban routes initially ran between Cleveland and Painesville. Starting in 1902, service between Painesville and Ashtabula operated as the Cleveland, Painesville, and Ashtabula line. The tracks ran through Madison along the south side of Main Street, as shown in this 1909 photograph. The interurban ceased operation in 1926, suffering from financial instability and the popularity of the automobile.

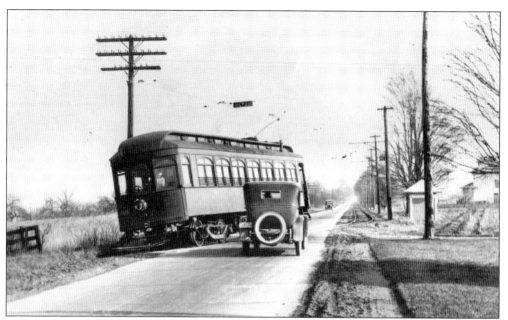

The interurban tracks crossed to the north side of South Ridge Road, traveling toward Perry west of Dayton Road. At that point, the tracks turned north and paralleled the Nickel Plate Railroad tracks. The small building at the right was stop 20. "Package car" streetcars also carried farm produce to Ashtabula to transfer onto railroad cars bound for Pittsburgh. Here a motorist waits for the streetcar to cross.

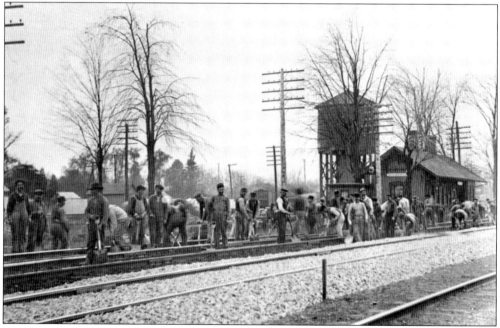

The first railroad locomotive passed through Madison in 1852, allowing people and goods to come and go much more easily. As in the rest of the United States, a flood of immigrants provided labor to build the railroad. This 1910 photograph, taken east of the Lake Street crossing, shows a crew working on the second track of the New York Central line.

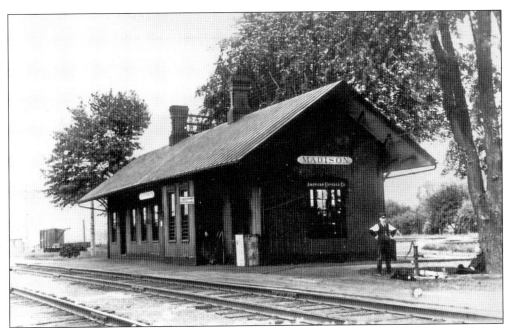

This 1909 photograph shows the Lake Shore and Michigan Southern (LSMS) depot. It was located on the south side of the tracks east of Lake Street. Posing near the water hand pump are station agent George Daugherty and Madison resident George Turney leaning against the tree. Note the American Express Company sign over the station window.

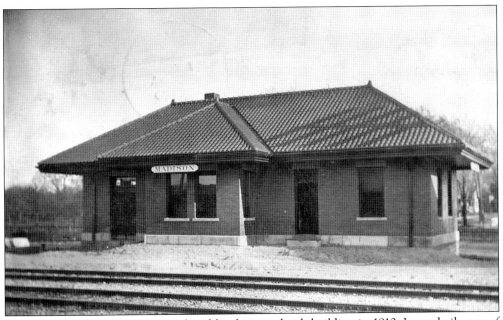

The wooden LSMS depot was replaced by this new brick building in 1910. It was built east of the old station near the end of Safford Street. The building represented the most modern of station facilities. The railroad "accommodation," or commuter train, provided efficient passenger transportation on the New York Central No. 601 run between Ashtabula and Cleveland. Commuter service was discontinued in 1936. The station was torn down in 1987.

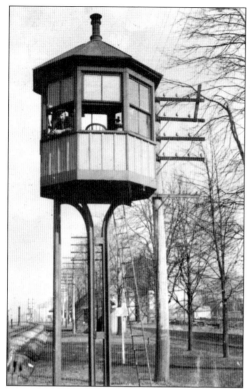

The railroad crossing guard was an important part of railroad operations. Safety gates at the crossing were lowered manually by a huge crank. The Madison New York Central railroad control tower was located on the south side of the tracks, east of the Lake Street crossing. The New York Central depot building stands in the background. Nickel Plate Railroad gate man William Gifford worked at the crossing from 1930 to 1935. Note the railroad watch pinned to his shirt. The crossing tower was torn down in 1947 when automatic gates were installed.

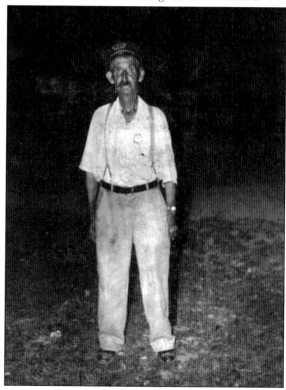

Inside the stations, operators manually threw switches to keep trains on the right track. In this photograph, Charles Luikart (center) and his fellow workers pause during work at the New York Central Railroad station in Madison. The New York Central's last commuter "accommodation" train ran on April 25, 1936. It was replaced by a Greyhound bus route, which ran between Ashtabula and the Cleveland Public Square.

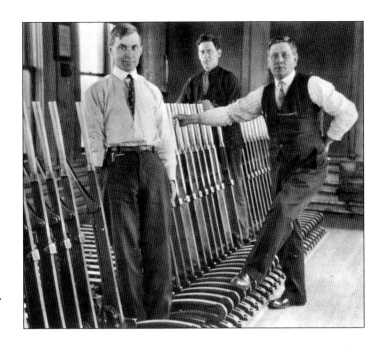

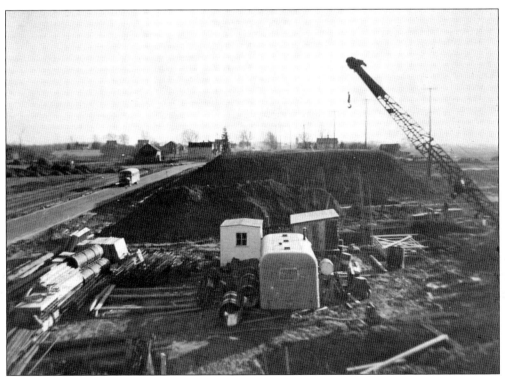

Roads in Madison gradually were changed from dirt to brick to concrete. In 1964, the State of Ohio constructed Interstate 90 traveling east and west across Ohio and Lake County. Madison's Route 528, River Street, became the location of Exit 212. Many family homes along this point were removed to make way for the wide span. Here construction on an entrance ramp is underway.

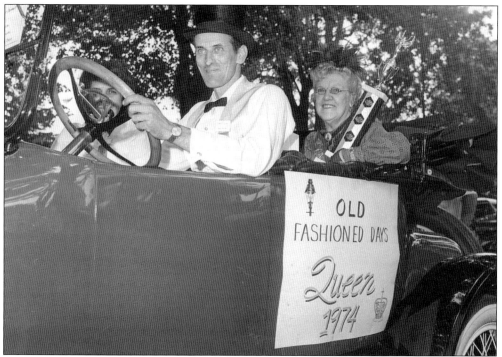

In 1974, a community-minded group of citizens created Madison Old Fashioned Days. The annual multiday event of parades, food, games, and dances still brings the community together and draws friends back to Madison for fun and memories. A past highlight of the event was choosing an Old Fashioned Days king and queen. Edith Rea, the first queen, is pictured here with driver Jesse Dowler and passenger Nellie Gragg.

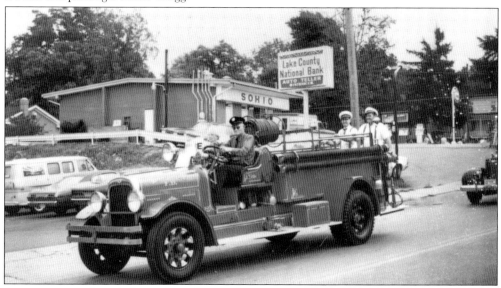

Antique cars and trucks have always been a favorite part of the Old Fashioned Days parade. In 1975, festival queen Alma Ritola rode down Lake Street in an antique Madison fire truck driven by George Spear, a Madison businessman and fireman. Riding on the back of the truck were Assistant Chief Wick R. Hathaway (left) and Chief Thomas E. Beattie.

Five

THE LAND'S BOUNTY

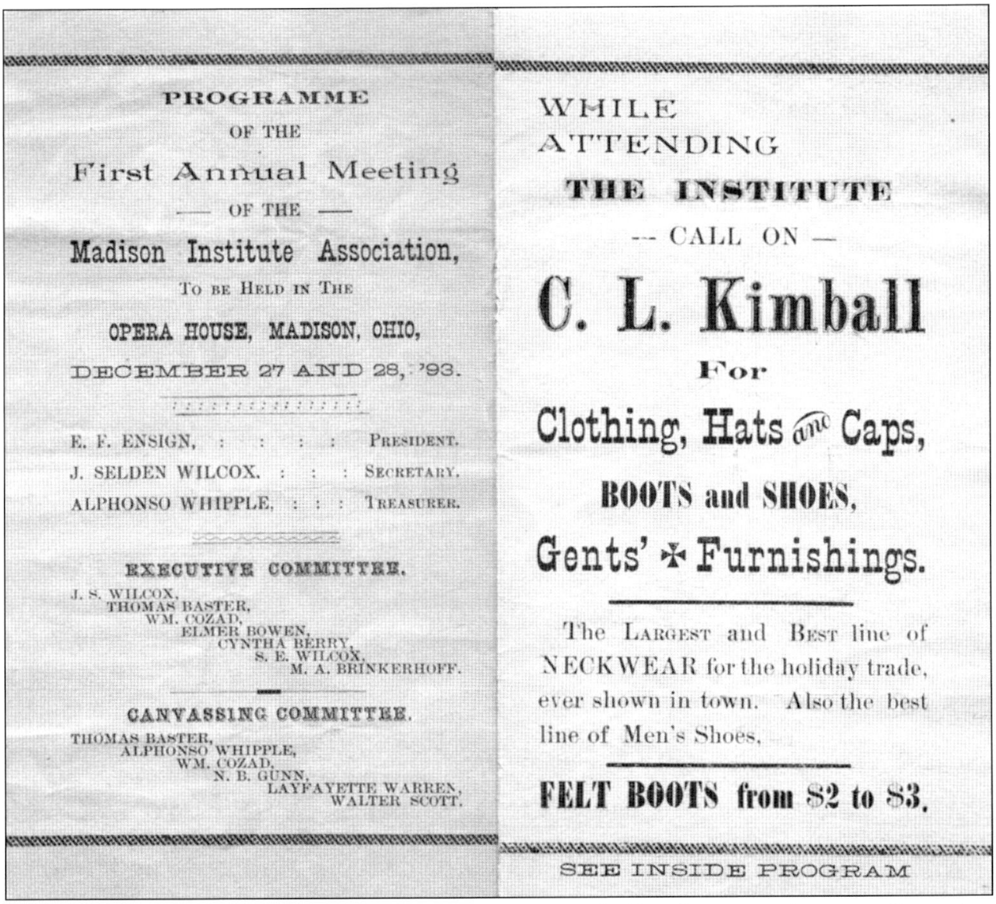

The Madison Farmers' Independent Institute Association held its first annual meeting December 27 and 28, 1893. For two days, farm families gathered at the Madison Opera House, upstairs in the Masonic Hall on Main Street, to hear speeches on good agricultural practices, musical entertainment, and cultural readings. Officers were E. F. Ensign, president; J. Seldon Wilcox, secretary; and Alphonso Whipple, treasurer. Pages two and three of the meeting program are shown here.

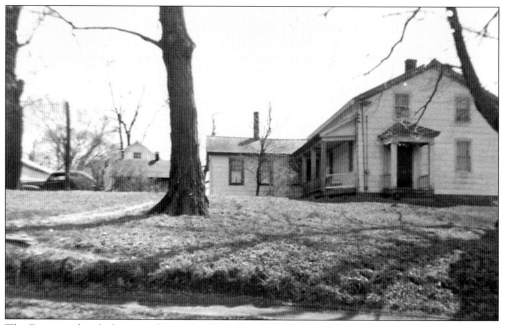

The Brewster family farm was located at 5320 South Ridge Road. Deacon Jasper Brewster came to Madison in 1812 and purchased a large tract of land. It stretched from the Ladd Tavern property to the border of the Fuller farm on the east. In 1816, Deacon Brewster built a brick home on the property, and later this frame house was built next door by his son Emerson Wadsworth Brewster.

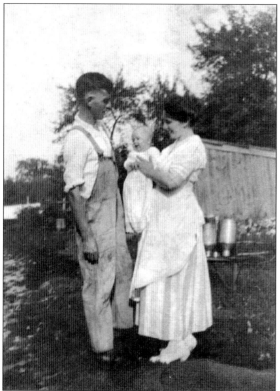

John Wadsworth Brewster and his wife, Julia Mary Hunt Brewster, proudly posed with the next generation on the family homestead. John was the great-grandson of Deacon Jasper Brewster. The Brewster farm raised hay, corn, wheat, and beans. A large herd of steers was raised for beef, along with cows, sheep, and hogs. The Brewster family farmed the acreage near their home for five generations.

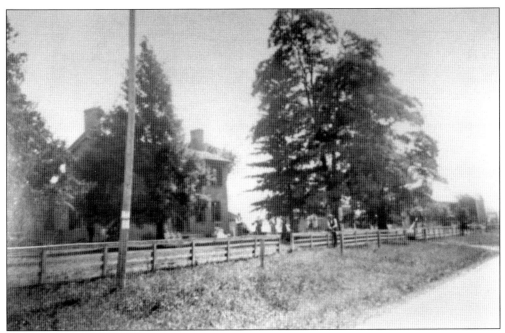

In 1840, John Sherwood purchased 163 acres on the western boundary of Madison Township, at 5288 South Ridge Road. He constructed a 17-room house from bricks that were made in a kiln on the property. The property was eventually sold to A. A. Amidon. In 1886, the property was purchased from the estate of A. A. Amidon by Frank Fuller of Cleveland.

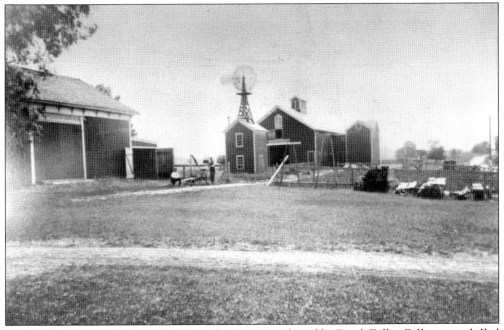

This 1890s photograph shows the farm after it was purchased by Frank Fuller. Fuller was a skilled carpenter who had done work on the Old Stone Church of Cleveland. New to farming, Fuller used his craft to further improve the farm. The Fuller farm was a model of efficiency, even yielding oil on the north side of the road. The Fullers often served on the Lake County Fair Board.

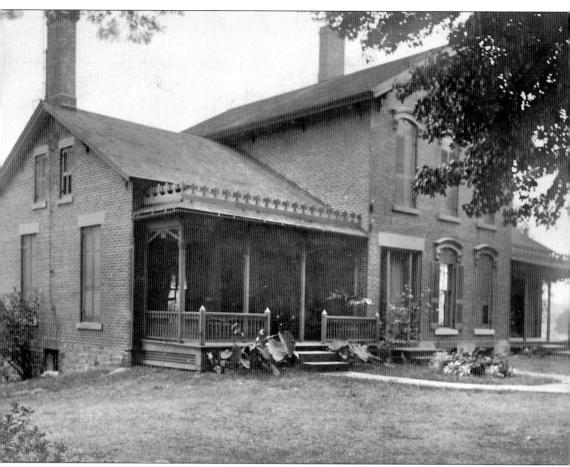

The farmhouse at 5582 South Ridge Road was built by Hezakiah Dewey between 1850 and 1853. The 120-acre farm was purchased by Andrew Rost in 1905. Rost raised potatoes and hay. He was one of the first farmers in Madison to use the railroad to transport his crops to Cleveland. In 1945, Charles Garrett, grandson of Andrew Rost, took over operation of the family farm. Garrett and his wife, Carol, developed a dairy business and later a chicken farm. At one time, the farm had 20,000 hens. The Rost-Garrett farm is still used for agriculture, its fields leased to a nursery company. The original house, post-and-beam barn, granary, and garage still stand on the property. The Garrett farm was designated Lake County's first Ohio Century Farm by the State of Ohio in 2009. The designation honors the farm's century-long contribution to the economic and cultural heritage of Ohio. (RR.)

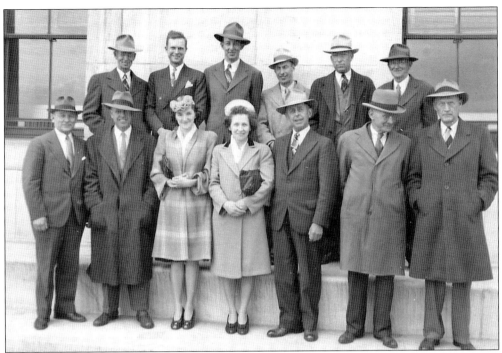

Charles and Carol Garrett were members of the Lake County Extension Advisors Committee. The extension service agent was Glenn Haskins. Tom Anderson of Madison was the soil conservationist. Shown about 1950, the first soil conservation advisors were, from left to right, (first row) Melvin Wyant, ? Spaulding, Carol Garrett, Elizabeth Komssi, ? Barber, ? Mantle, and ? Quigley; (second row) ? Plaisted, Charles Garrett, Earl Komssi, Russell Adams, Ralph Taylor, and ? Webster.

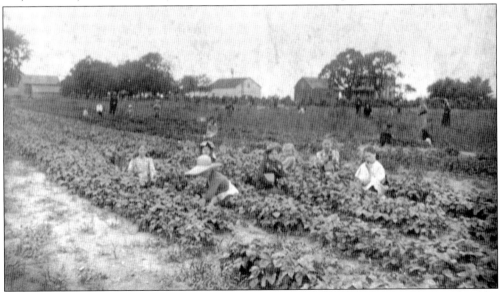

In 1877, the Hathaway family established Fertile Acres Farms on the south side of South Ridge Road west of Dayton Road. Wick Hathaway specialized in wholesale berry plants and purebred poultry. This photograph of a strawberry harvest was used as the basis for a cartoon drawing in one of Hathaway's many product catalogs. (CH.)

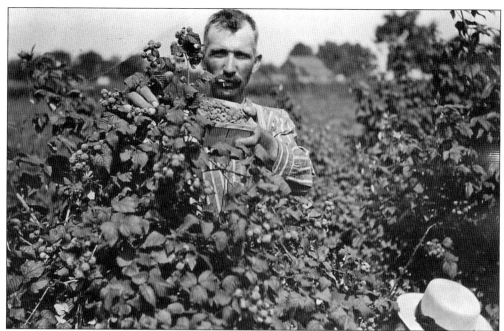

Here Wick Hathaway poses with his Columbian raspberry plants. Wick was active in many agricultural groups, wrote books on agricultural methods, and promoted his products with gusto. He sold the Wick Hathaway Hundred Dollar and Money Maker varieties of strawberries, as well as blackberries, currants, gooseberries, grapevines, fruit trees, and onion seed. (CH.)

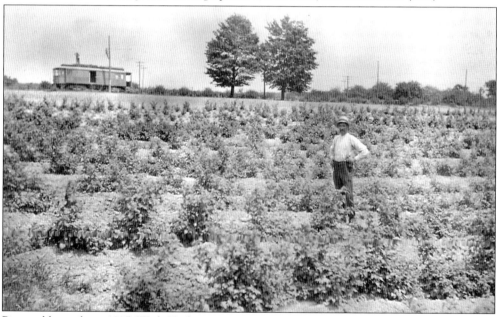

Pictured here about 1915, Wick Hathaway poses in a field of berry bushes while the interurban streetcar pulls up to stop 20. Wick also ventured into poultry breeding and sales. He produced a series of booklets with pen-and-ink drawings showing a multitude of poultry varieties. Hathaway Brothers advertising promoted their "$20,000.00 hen coop" in Unionville, an ornate building claimed to be 535 feet long. (CH.)

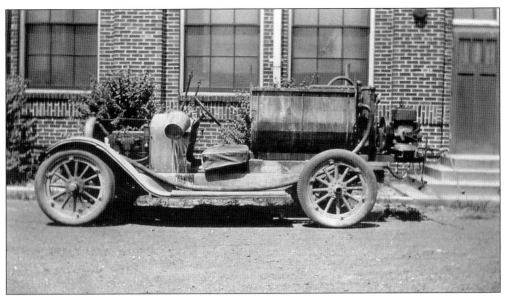

In 1928, the Madison High School vocational agriculture students sprayed crops. The spray rig used by the agriculture club was mounted on a Chevrolet truck. The club sprayed potatoes, apple orchards, grapes, and other seasonal crops with the outfit. The all-boy group was advised by Madison High School instructor Glenn Haskins.

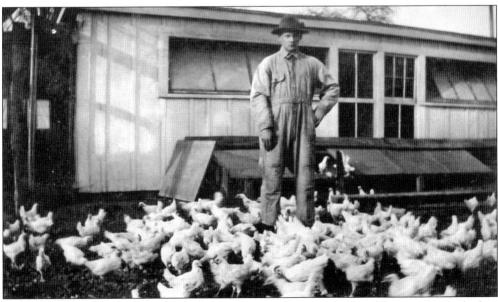

The Madison High School agricultural club also studied raising poultry. The organization had an annual egg and poultry show in connection with the Farmers Institute, with exhibits at the high school. In 1928, enrollment in the agricultural course and the club were still increasing. Here Martin Rand, a student in the program, poses at the Middle Ridge Hatchery west of Bates Road.

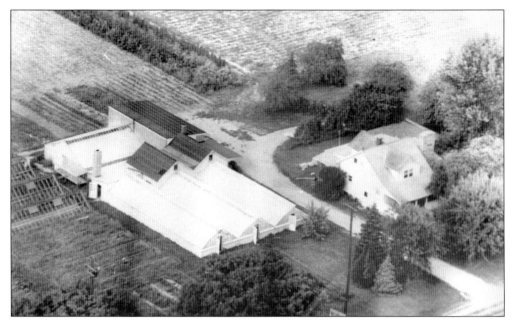

Martin Rand (descendant of the pioneer Martin Rand) and his wife, Imogene, established a farm on the north side of Middle Ridge Road, just east of Burns Road. The farm was known as Madison Gardens. Their greenhouses grew flowers and specialized in African violets. The aerial view shows neatly plowed fields, greenhouses, and the family home. The buildings and greenhouses were removed for condominiums in the 1990s.

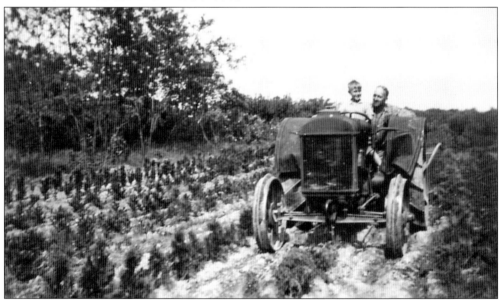

The Lake County nursery business was established in 1857. The excellent growing conditions soon made Lake County the nation's largest nursery center. In 1927, thirty-six charter members formed the Lake County Nurserymen's Association. In 1943, Jacob Turkenburg established J. Turkenburg Nurseries on South Wood Road in Madison. The nursery specialized in evergreens, hollies, azaleas, lilacs, and rhododendrons. Seen here in 1946, Jacob and his son Dick ride on their Fordson tractor. (PT.)

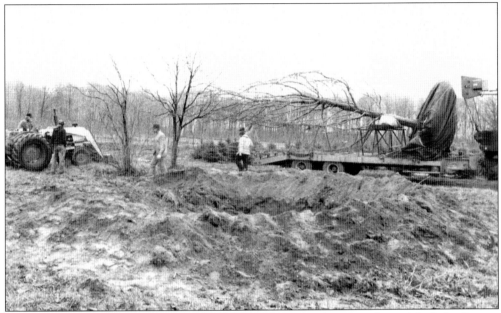

Today nursery fields fill Madison Township. In the 1950s, Madison members of the Lake County Nurserymen's Association were the Cook Place—Ivan D. Cook; CZ Nurseries; Green Ridge Nursery—Alan Cook; Greenwood Nursery—Charles A. Brotzman; and Ridgeview Nursery—Ralph E. Harper, Jacob Turkenburg, and William S. Noe. In this 1982 photograph, a large tree is being removed from a field at Brotzmans Nursery, Inc. (BN-PD.)

The Lake County Nurserymen's Association focuses on promoting best agricultural practices and sharing information on advancing the science. In this photograph taken in 1982, Tim Brotzman (left) and his father, Charles Brotzman, both past presidents of the Lake County Nurserymen's Association, inspect the roots of a maple tree at the family nursery at 6899 Chapel Road. (BN-PD.)

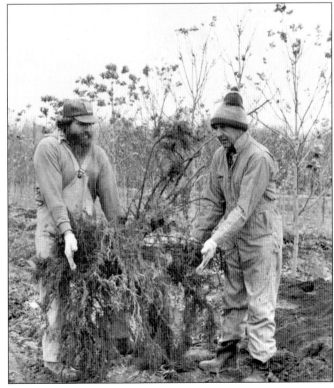

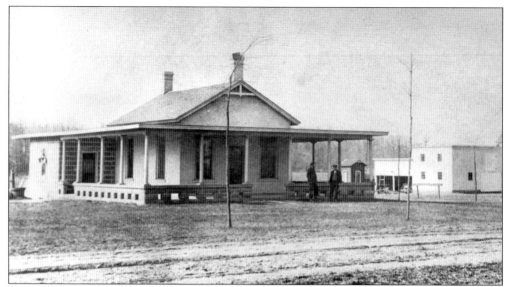

This house at 7024 Middle Ridge Road was originally a schoolhouse owned by the Madison Township School District. In 1899, it was sold to Miles C. Rathbun. In 1903, a porch was added, according to the cornerstone inscription, and additions were built at the back. In the 1960s, when the farm was owned by the Richard Belknap family, the porch was removed and the brick exterior restored.

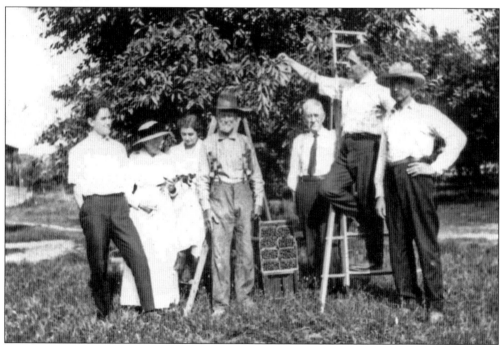

In 1909, Miles Rathbun sold the farm at 7024 Middle Ridge Road to Mary Watkins. The Watkins family continued to expand the farm. Here the cherry harvest is proudly displayed in their orchard. Later, under the ownership of the Belknaps, the farm's produce was sold at a roadside stand. The farm produced apples, cherries, peaches, grapes, gooseberries, black and red raspberries, strawberries, rhubarb, and seasonal vegetables.

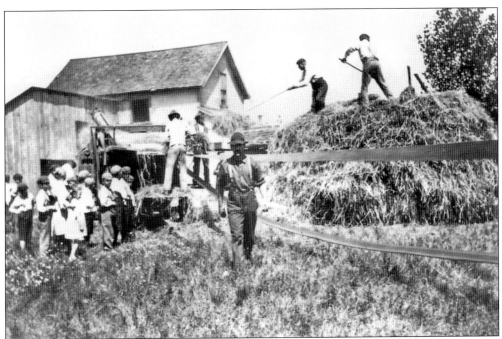

An interested group of children watches as hay is processed by farm machinery on the Watkins farm. The corn crib and tractor barn were removed by the Belknap family in the late 1960s and 1970s. The large barn was removed in the late 1970s. Today the wide fields have returned to wooded property.

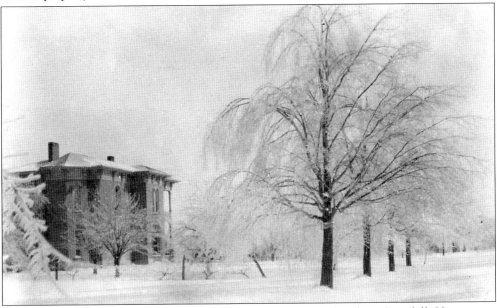

Sunnyside Farm at 7125 Middle Ridge Road was owned by Theodore Crandall. His parents came by oxcart to Madison from Connecticut in 1823. The large brick home was designed and constructed in 1873 by his father-in-law, Lyman Maltby. Sunnyside Farm had apple orchards and vineyards and produced Crandall's specialty, Rareripe peaches. This photograph shows the home covered with ice following the storm of February 14, 1909. (RR.)

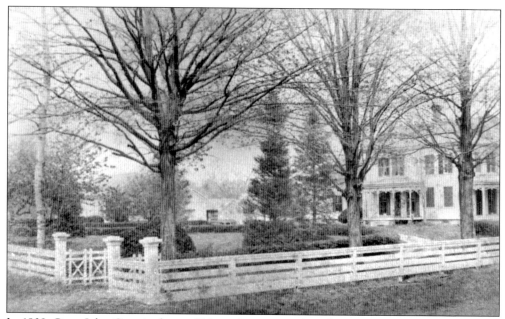

In 1809, Capt. John Cunningham of Massachusetts purchased 2,699 acres that extended from Middle Ridge Road to the Lake Erie shore along the east boundary of Madison Township. In 1813, he built a frame house near his original log cabin at the intersection of County Line and Middle Ridge Roads. This photograph, taken about 1900, is of the home believed to be Cunningham's at 7831 Middle Ridge Road.

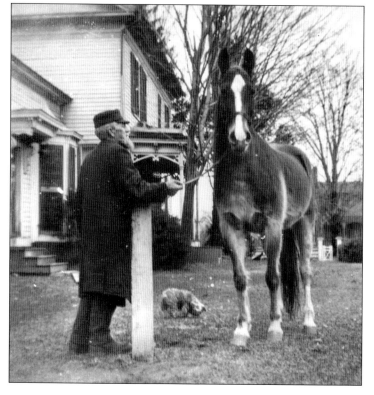

The great-granddaughter of Captain Cunningham, Evaline Ladd Cunningham, married William E. Hulett (pictured here). Evaline and William lived in the Cunningham family home on Middle Ridge. Hulett was the brother of George H. Hulett, inventor of the Hulett Unloading Machine. The giant machines were used to unload ore boats at Great Lakes ports. Prior to moving to Cleveland in 1881, George Hulett owned a general store in Unionville.

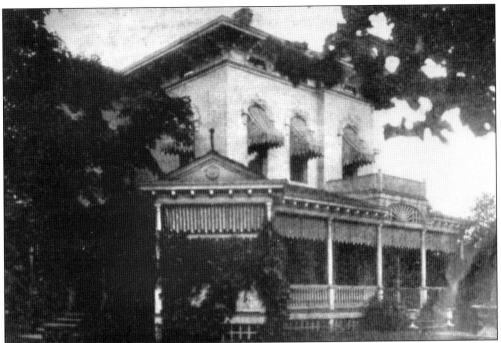

Unionville cooper George H. Hopper amassed a fortune after perfecting a traveling tramp's formula to seal barrels, according to local legend. Hopper obtained a contract to supply Rockefeller's Standard Oil Company with barrels and was able to replace his simple house with this mansion at 3142 County Line Road. Hopper enjoyed breeding horses and entertained the elite at his own racetrack on the property.

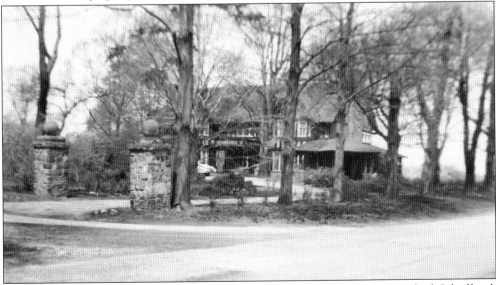

George Hopper's daughter Jennie Marie married Frederic M. Nicholas, a Standard Oil official. They built this estate on a portion of the Hopper land at the north corner of Middle Ridge and County Line Roads. They named their estate Broadfields. The date 1903 is carved in the chimney. The property had its own golf course. Frederic Nicholas, well known in Cleveland society, helped organize the Cleveland Hermit and Singers Clubs.

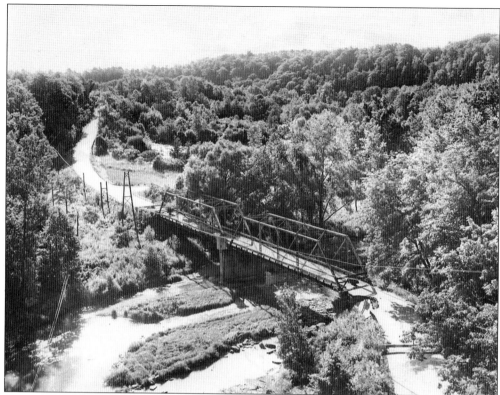

Crossing into south Madison Township required crossing the Grand River. The King Bridge Company of Cleveland constructed this iron bridge connecting Klasen and Bailey Roads in 1893. At that time, the two roads were both part of Madison Road. Only the original stone abutments and central piling still remain along the river in Hidden Valley Park. The old Grand River Bridge was replaced by a high-level bridge in 1962.

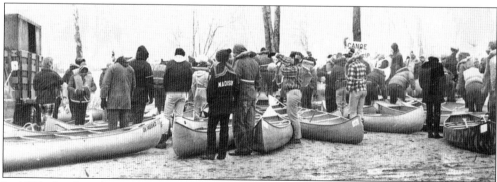

In 1974, the Grand River was designated a State Wild and Scenic River. Beginning in 1964, it was the setting for outdoor fun in the form of the Mad Hatters Canoe Race. The race ran from Harpersfield Dam to Hidden Valley Metropark in Madison. A "maddest hat contest" was a highlight of the event. This photograph from the early 1970s shows participants waiting for results at the race's finish. (AG.)

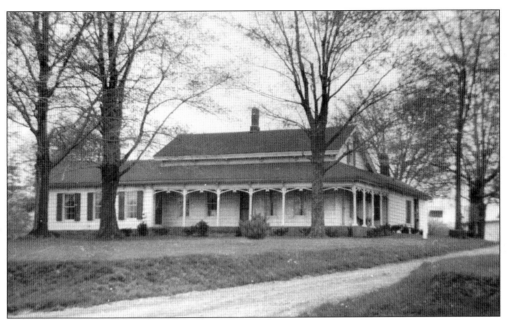

Col. Luther Trumbull came to Madison from Groton, New York, in 1827. He built this house at the corner of Griswold Road and Route 528, south of the Grand River. He owned a gristmill, a sawmill, and a cloth mill. Trumbull hired Homer Griswold, a talented weaver, to run the cloth mill. Griswold married Trumbull's daughter, Laura, who inherited the homestead when her father died in 1840. (BW.)

In 1910, Paul and Gertrude Faust purchased the 138-acre Trumbull-Griswold property. Faust, a talented carpenter, restored the house and farm. He had the reputation of having the highest yield per acre of grain of any farmer in the area. The Fausts, who also operated a grocery store in South Madison, are pictured at their home in the 1960s. Today the house lies empty on the Thunderhill Golf Club property. (BW.)

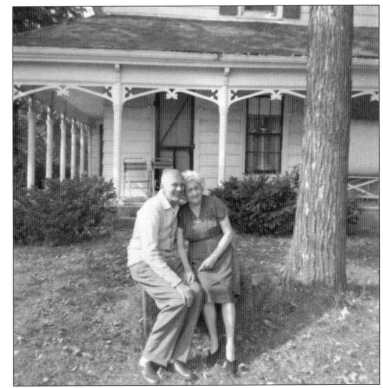

Taste **GRISWOLD'S** *Once*

100% Pure

Maple Sugar

America's Greatest Delicacy

FIVE POUNDS NET WT.

"Eat and Be Sweet Honey"

Manufactured and Distributed by

GRISWOLD HONEY CO.
MADISON, OHIO, U. S. A.

Sap from Ohio's sugar maples has provided sugar since the first settlers arrived. A descendant of Homer Griswold, Gerald Griswold, produced popular maple and honey products during the 1930s. Gerald Griswold lived in Madison Village on West Main Street. Here is a label from his maple sugar. A 1935 *Directory of Madison, Ohio* advertisement calls his products "The World's Best Health Sweets."

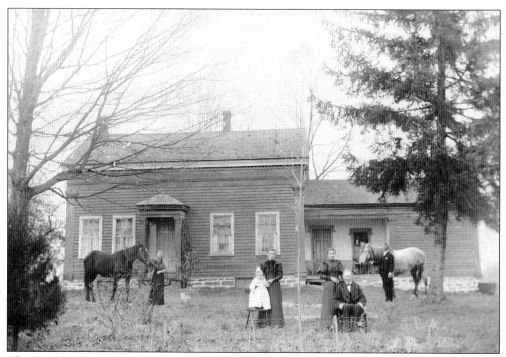

The Ross family came from Antrim, Ireland, and settled in south Madison Township along a portion of the old Western Reserve Girdled Road, which became Ross Road. Samuel J. Ross purchased the homestead from his uncle William Ross in 1890. Samuel is pictured with his horse; William is seated at the right. Others pictured are, from left to right, Agnes Ross, Howard Ross (the child), Lida Ross, and Margaret Ross.

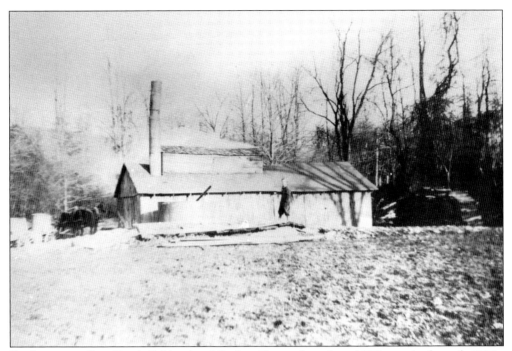

Farther east on Ross Road, Gebhard and Pauline Hummel purchased 300 acres in the early 1900s. Leaving his business as a brass smelter in Cleveland, Hummel and his sons established a farm on the property that extended into Ashtabula County. Here is the sugar bush they built on the property. The family farm still produces maple syrup; the old sugar bush has now been replaced by a modern operation. (MS.)

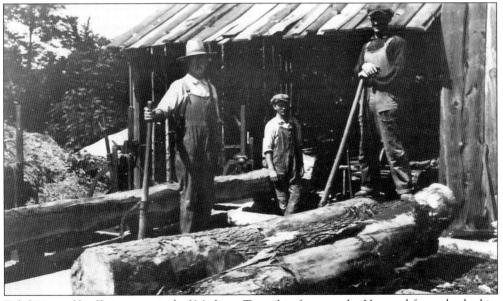

Exhibiting self-sufficiency typical of Madison Township farmers, the Hummel farm also had its own sawmill. Hummel cleared timber from his property, which is still done today, to heat the stoves for maple syrup production and provide home heating fuel and building lumber. Shown at the sawmill are, from left to right, Gebhard, Joe, and Arnold Hummel. (MS.)

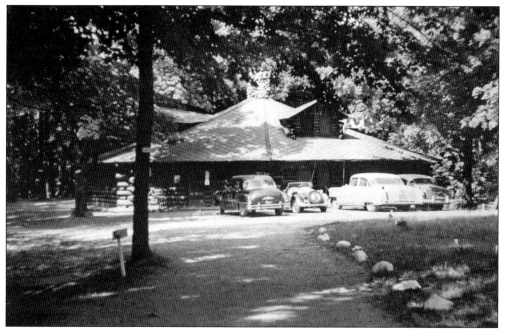

In 1930, the Northeast Ohio Council of the Boy Scouts of America purchased about 127 acres (which would become 350) on Ross Road. It became Camp Stigwandish. As part of construction, logs were hauled in by horse and wagon to build an octagonal log dining hall. The hall was dismantled in 1956 and replaced. The camp has created outdoor memories for thousands of northeast Ohio Boy Scouts. (EH.)

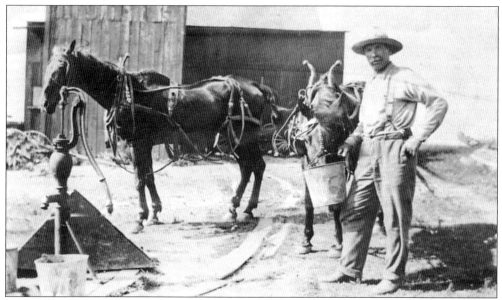

In 1845, Reuben Ford and his wife, Climena Vrooman Ford, established a homestead in South Madison on what would become Ford Road. By 1853, Ford had accumulated 274 acres. The 1869 *Painesville Telegraph* reported that wool from his farm "brought the highest figure yet paid in this market and several cents more than buyers are paying in Cleveland." Here Reuben Ford poses with his team of horses. (AG.)

In 1891, the widowed Climena Ford sold the family farm to one of her sons, Elisha, "for a consideration of $500." Children at the Ford farm were taught a love of the land and animals. Seen around 1916, Garrett Ford and Alberta Scott (in the wagon) play with Billy the goat and their own cart. The homestead has remained in the family to this day, through seven generations. (AG.)

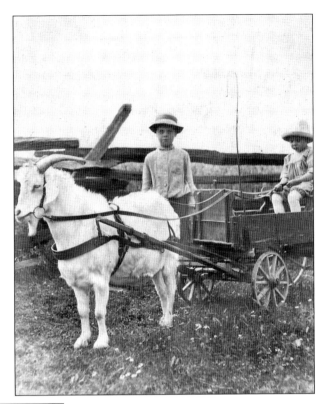

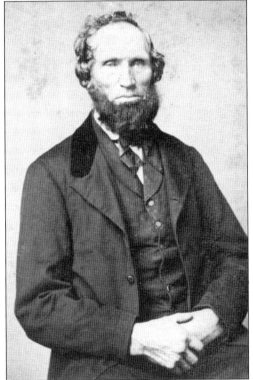

Harmon Doty, shown here, was born in Perry, Ohio, in 1833 to Lymon Doty and Louise Harris. An 1857 map of Madison shows Lymon owned land south of the Grand River, east of Emerson Road. An 1870 property map of Madison shows Harmon as the owner of a 63-acre tract of land south of his father's. The road on which they owned property has become Doty Road.

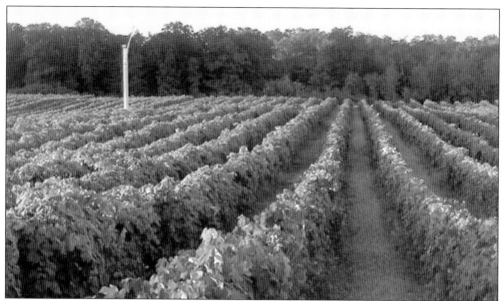

Along Doty Road today, vineyards dominate the landscape. This 2006 view of Debonne Vineyards shows evidence of the fine soil and climate that give rise to the wine-producing industry in northeastern Ohio. The moderating climate provided by Lake Erie offers some protection from crop-damaging frosts. However, wind machines are also installed—just in case. (DV.)

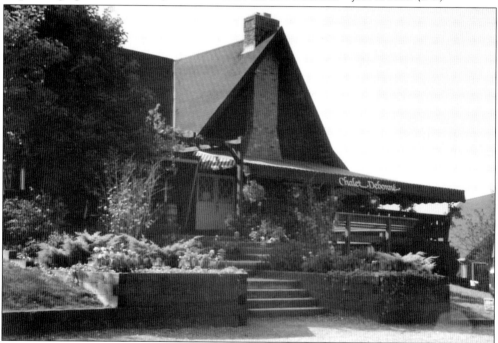

Debonne Vineyards began operations in 1971 as the Debevec family business. Anthony Debevec Jr. returned from Ohio State University with a degree in pomology in 1969. He and his father, Anthony Debevec Sr., combined modern agricultural methods with the winemaker's art. Their original chalet on Doty Road is pictured here in 1990. Several award-winning wineries now operate in Madison and the surrounding area. (DV.)

Six

THE LURE OF THE LAKE

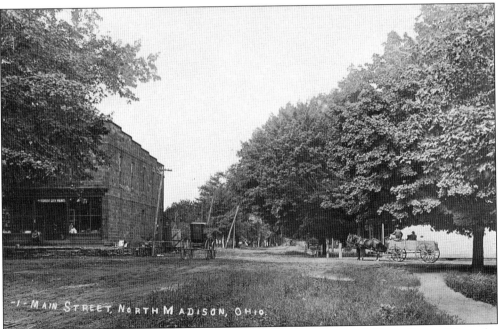

This view is of North Madison looking west on North Ridge Road (State Route 20) at the intersection of Hubbard Road. This intersection was originally called Branch's Corners, after William Branch, who settled here in 1837. The store on the left is the Edward J. Davet store, which dealt in groceries and general merchandise. The sign over the door advertises Forest City Paints. Davet opened his store in 1903.

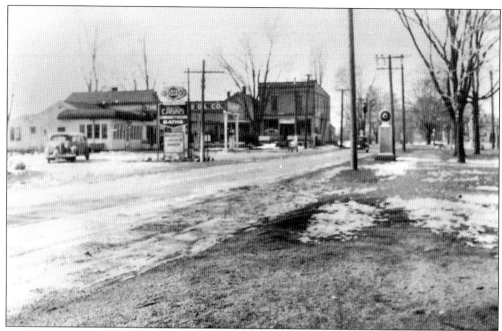

A 1930s view of the North Ridge and Hubbard Roads intersection shows the old Edward J. Davet store, which was then owned by the Quirk family. By this time, the North Ridge Road had been paved in brick. Note the manual stop signal located on the right side of the road. A Standard Oil Company station was on the southeast corner, next to the Cabins restaurant.

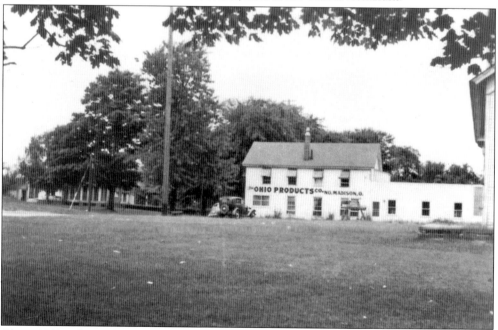

About 1868, Jules and Joseph Davet built a blacksmith shop at 2649 Hubbard Road, just north of North Ridge Road. The shop produced the first wheel hoe used in Madison Township. In this 1941 photograph, the building had become the Ohio Products Company, owned by Robert and Gordon Quirk. On the far right, the first Congregational Church is barely visible.

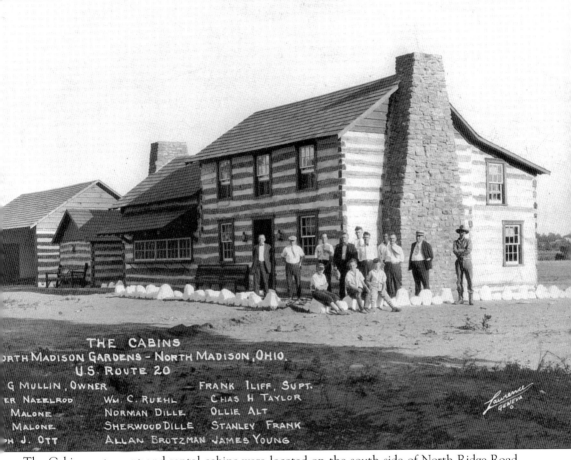

THE CABINS

JRTH MADISON GARDENS – NORTH MADISON, OHIO.
U.S. ROUTE 20

G MULLIN, OWNER — FRANK ILIFF, SUPT.
ER NAZELROD   WM. C. RUEHL   CHAS H TAYLOR
MALONE   NORMAN DILLE   OLLIE ALT
MALONE   SHERWOOD DILLE   STANLEY FRANK
'H J. OTT   ALLAN BROTZMAN JAMES YOUNG

The Cabins restaurant and rental cabins were located on the south side of North Ridge Road just east of Hubbard Road. The cabin building was originally constructed elsewhere and moved to Madison about 1928 by Carl Mullin. The Cabins restaurant building was removed in 1955 to make room for a shopping center. Names listed on the photograph are Carl G. Mullin, Walter Nazelrod, John Malone, Fred Malone, Joseph Ott, William C. Ruehl, Norman Dille, Sherwood Dille, Allan Brotzman, Supt. Frank Iliff, Charles H. Taylor, Ollie Alt, Stanley Frank, and James Young. The photograph is labeled "North Madison Gardens," which was the building lot development behind the restaurant.

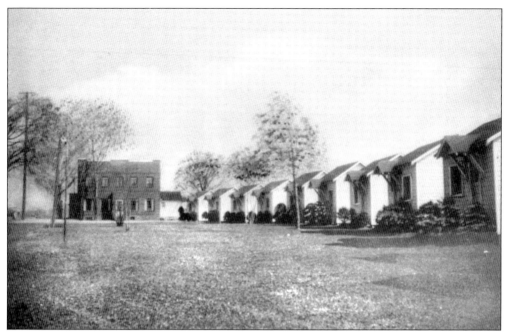

The automobile brought an increasing number of travelers through Madison along North Ridge Road. Branch's Circle Inn, according to this postcard, provided many travelers' services. The large brick building offered a "modern restaurant and open air dining room, serving 80–100 breakfasts and dinners daily." The property also had "23 deluxe cabins, apartments, duplex, single units, steam heat, tile baths, [and] garages." (RR.)

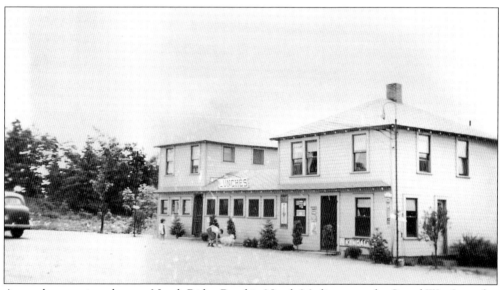

A popular stopping place on North Ridge Road in North Madison was the Speed Way Inn, also known as "Hungry Hubby? So Am I." The small restaurant and gas station was operated by V. C. Warren. It was located just east of Burns Road on Route 20. Other restaurants and cabins cropped up along Route 20, including Ridge Lunch, Oster's Inn, Hatch's Rock Garden, and Locust Grove. (RR.)

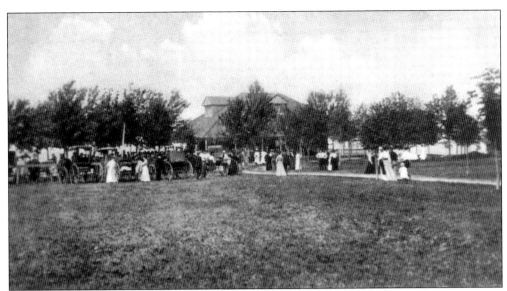

The Lake Erie shore has always presented economic, cultural, and entertainment opportunities. As early as July 4, 1813, a community picnic was held at Phineas Mixer's cabin at the shore. The tradition continued with the Madison Harvest Festival, which took place at the Madison Township Park in Madison on the Lake. This 1907 photograph shows the festival crowd arriving in their buggies near the park pavilion.

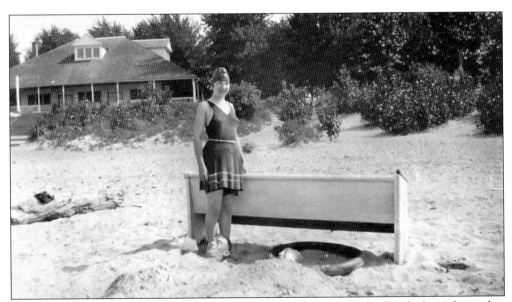

The Madison Township Park pavilion was the center of activity at the beach. Its wide porches provided shade for lounging, and dances and parties were held inside. The pavilion was built in 1905 and used through 1933, when it burned down. This photograph of an unidentified bather and her sand-buried friends was taken about 1925.

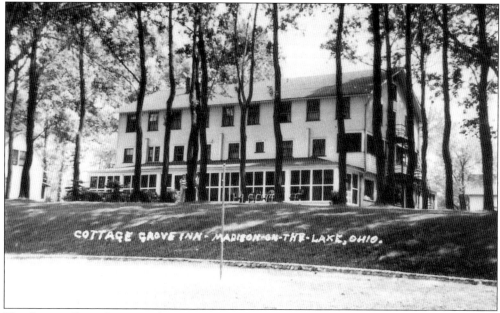

The Cottage Grove Inn invited summer visitors to relax and enjoy the Lake Erie shore at Madison on the Lake. The large inn, located just east of Madison Township Park, was built in 1914 by Judd W. Snell. Snell operated the Park Hotel in Madison Village from 1902 to 1915.

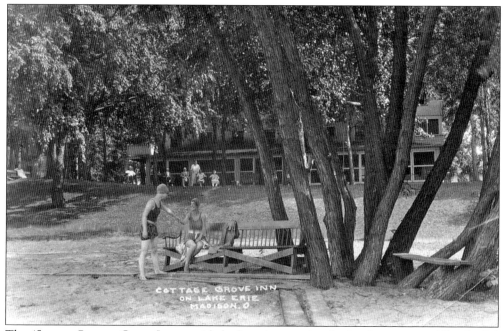

The 45-room Cottage Grove Inn provided a luxurious setting for family vacations. The shaded lawn and beach overlooked Lake Erie. This postcard is postmarked 1928. The hotel remained under the operation of the Snell family until it closed. The hotel building was demolished in 1962 when the land was allotted for homes.

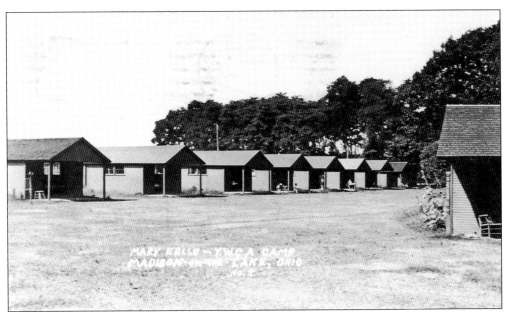

In 1912, the Young Women's Christian Association of Cleveland purchased 80 acres on Chapel Road along Lake Erie's shore. The purchase was funded by Mrs. Daniel P. (Mary) Eells and was named the Mary Eells Vacation Farm in her honor. The camp accommodated 125 high school–aged girls who attended for two-week sessions. Separate sessions were also offered for "employed girls." This view of the cabins was taken in 1935.

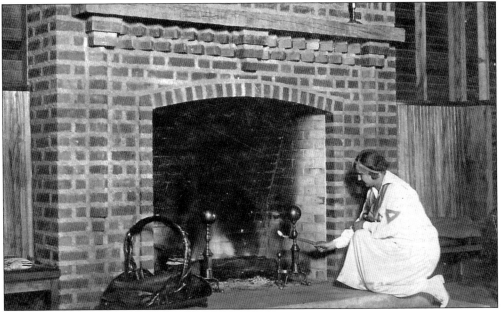

Camp attendees wrote home on postcards showing views of the camp. One card had the printed slogan, "Where Health and Playtime Meet." Activities at Mary Eells Vacation Farm included horseback riding, swimming, and tennis lessons. The bungalow provided a central meeting spot for activities. A uniformed camp leader lights the fireplace in the bungalow shown on this postcard dated 1925.

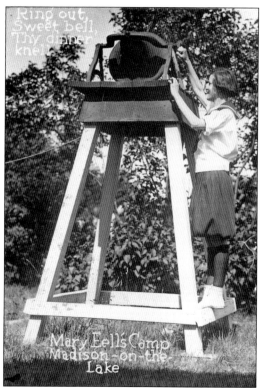

The camp was also a working farm that produced food for the campers. A 1921 camper wearing the Mary Eells uniform—middy blouse, bloomers, stockings, and high-topped shoes—rings the dinner bell. The YWCA sold the camp to the Catholic Diocese, and it was renamed Camp Isaac Jogues. In 1998, Madison Township purchased the property, which was dedicated as Bill Stanton Community Park on April 25, 1999. (RR.)

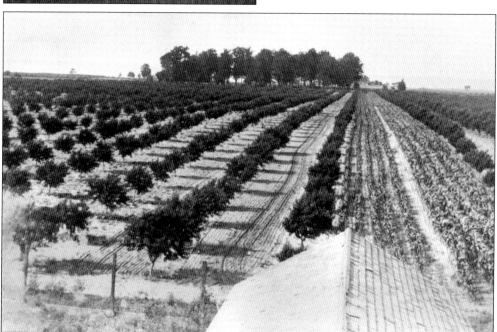

In the 1920s, land developers recognized the potential building value of the land along the Lake Erie shoreline. Landowners along the lake were approached to sell the wide fields they used as nurseries and orchards. This photograph shows the fields between Hubbard and Bennett Roads that would become the Cumings Beach Park development.

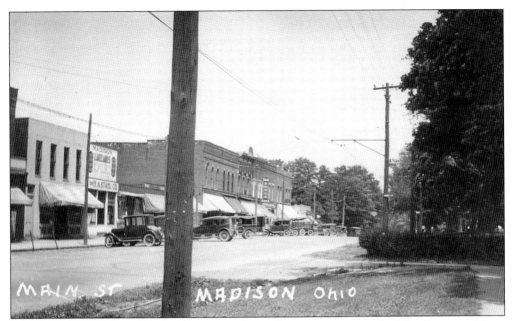

On Main Street in the village, realtors set up shop selling property along the lake. Summer visitors to Madison were potential buyers of summer homes. Visitors came from Cleveland, Warren, Pittsburgh, and beyond to enjoy the Madison shore. This 1920s photograph shows the large sign erected by H. A. Stahl Company promoting the Madison Golf Lakelands development, which included what is today the Madison Country Club.

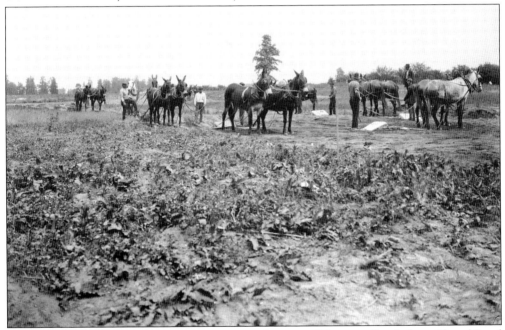

In 1920, H. A. Stahl Properties Company invested in over 500 acres of land along Chapel Road extending to the lake and named it the Madison Golf Lakelands. Stahl cleared the land for hundreds of homesites and a golf course. Here a photograph from his promotional materials describes, "20 mule teams busy converting 500 acres into a wonderful summer home development." (MCC.)

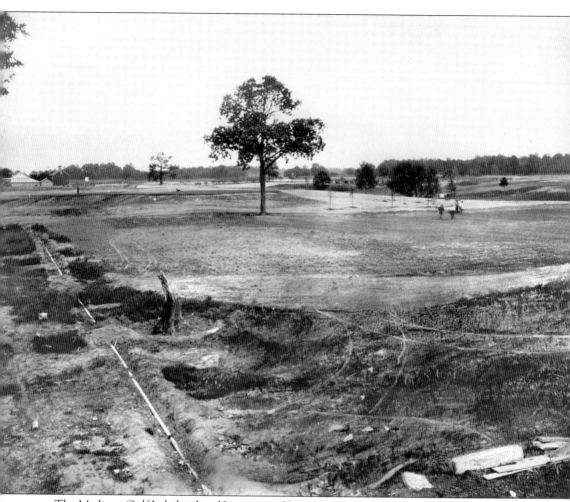

The Madison Golf Lakelands golf course on Chapel Road was started in September 1921. Grange Alves was the golf course designer, and his brother William Alves was the first golf professional when the course opened. Shown above and at the right is a panoramic view of the Chapel Road golf course while under construction. (MCC.)

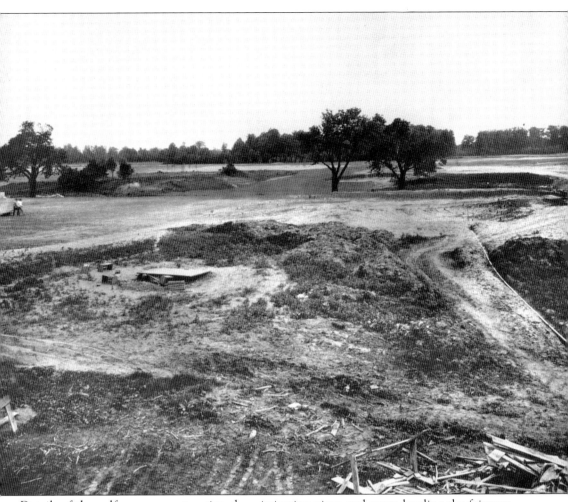

Details of the golf course construction show irrigation pipes and crews leveling the fairways. On the south side of the road, the men's locker room, a grill, and pro shop would be built. In 1925, a nine-hole course was also opened on Route 20. The construction of the short course was supervised by Stanley Aldrich, who remained on as the first groundskeeper for Madison Golf Lakelands. (MCC.)

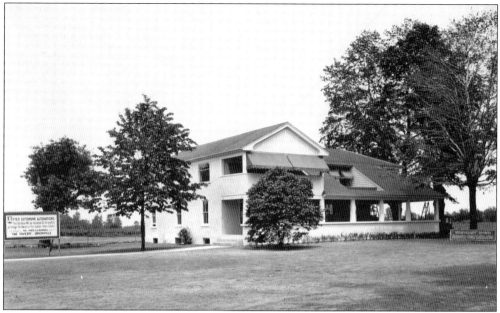

This 1920 photograph shows the Madison Golf Lakelands office at 6131 Chapel Road. The sign reads, "After extensive alterations this club house will be maintained for the benefit of all cottage site owners in this summer home colony. To be managed by Mr. & Mrs. G. A. Randall formerly of 'The Tavern' of Unionville." This building, once the Chubb family home, became part of the Madison Country Club clubhouse. (MCC.)

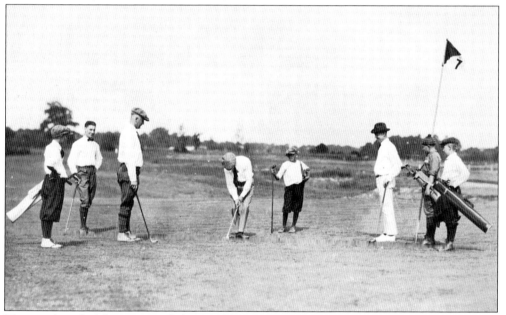

This unidentified foursome and their caddies are enjoying the seventh hole at the Madison Golf Lakelands course in the early 1920s. Members of the club had to be property owners in the Madison Golf Lakelands and pay a $10 initiation fee and $10 in annual dues; greens fees were $1. In 1950, club rules were changed so that members no longer were required to be Golf Lakelands property owners. (MCC.)

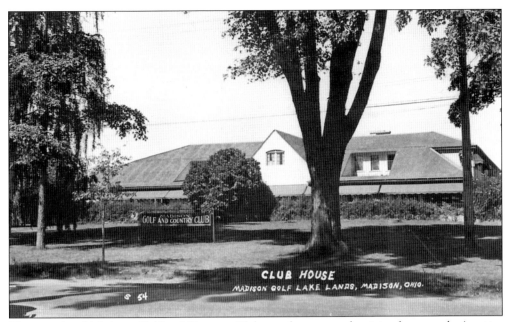

The completed Madison Golf and Country Club was the center of activity for a member's entire family. There was a children's day camp, three dances a week, game night, and weekly movies. In 1962, the Madison Golf Lakelands became the Madison Country Club. Activities and improvements have continued to the present day. (RR.)

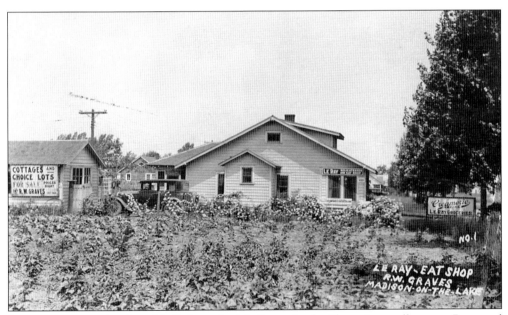

Property continued to be sold all along the lakefront. At the Shore Acres allotment, Raymond W. Graves advertised the sale of "Cottages and Choice Lots, Prices Right." Graves also had a multipurpose business operating the Le Ray Eat Shop. He operated a grocery store, delicatessen, and ice cream shop out of the bungalow. (RR.)

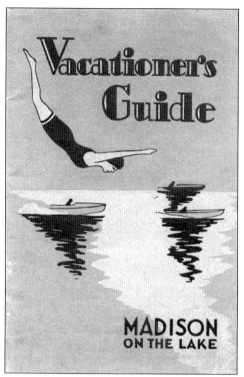

The Lake Erie shore became filled with summer cottages sold and rented to vacationers. In 1931, the Boosters Club of Madison published this *Vacationer's Guide*. It provided information for visitors such as the train and bus schedules and advertising for local businesses. Entertainment options included the Golf Lakeland polo fields and swimming and tennis at Madison Township Park.

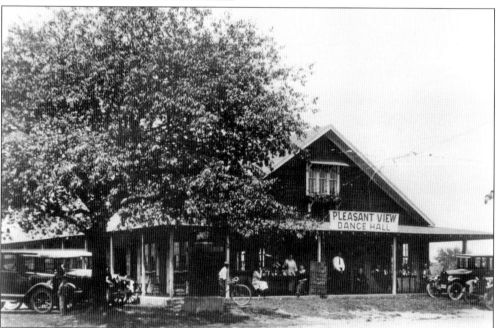

The intersection where Hubbard Road ended at the lake became the center of entertainment for Madison on the Lake. The township park was surrounded by activities and services catering to summer visitors. The Pleasant View Dance Hall was one of the earliest commercial ventures. The location would later be known as the Park View Dance Hall when it advertised that Hal Lynn's Orchestra appeared all season.

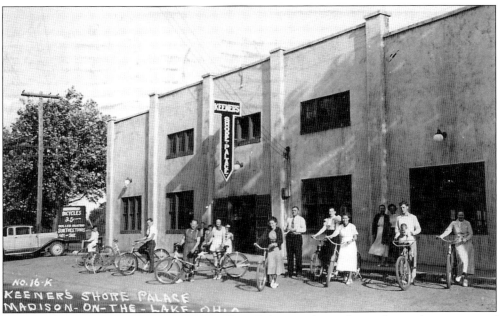

Operated by G. Keener and Sons, Keener's Shore Palace was located near the southeast corner of Hubbard and Lake Roads across the street from the Madison Township Park. The 1935 *Directory of Madison, Ohio* advertised the "modern equipped roller rink and dance pavilion," which also rented bicycles. The Shore Palace was a meeting place and entertainment center for local residents and summer visitors.

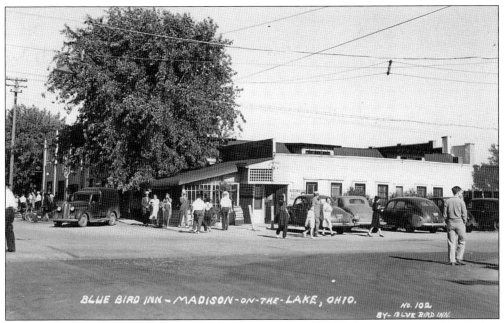

Next door to Keener's Shore Palace was the Blue Bird Inn. The restaurant was owned by Arthur and Hulda Fritz, who also operated the Unionville Old Tavern. Other owners were John Ritola and Fred Ellis. An advertisement for the Blue Bird Inn promoted its sandwiches, chicken, and steak dinners. They urged patrons to "try our Sweetheart Waffles and Homemade Pie."

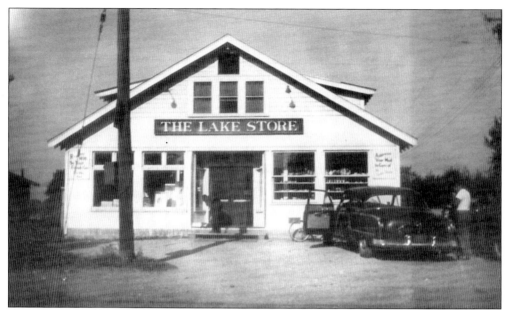

John and Alma Ritola operated the Lake Store, a small grocery store at the end of Hubbard Road. The store was a central operating point for many visitors. The sign on the right side of the building encourages customers to "address your mail in care of the Lake Store" so they could pick up correspondence while on vacation.

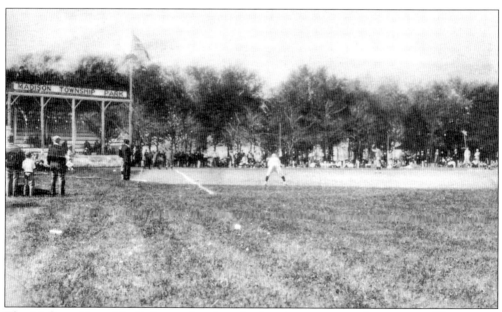

The Madison Township Park was the place for dancing, tennis, and swimming. There was a bathhouse where, in 1931, swimsuits could be rented for 35¢ with no time limit for the day. The baseball diamond formed the center of the park. This 1941 postcard shows the stands and a game in action.

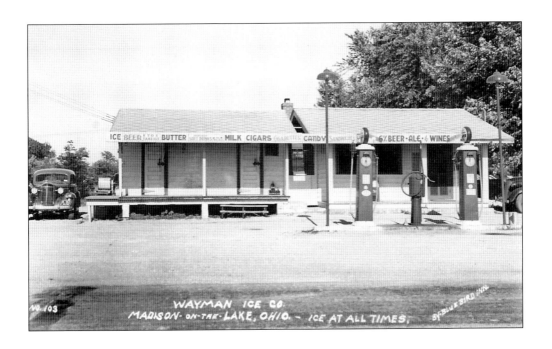

L. J. Wayman owned the Wayman Ice Company in Madison-on-the-Lake. It was the place to fuel up and buy milk, candy, beer, wine, and ice for coolers. The Wayman Ice Company sponsored a tug-of-war team at the August 18, 1937, Harvest Festival. They were pitted against the Cleveland Rams football team. The powerful Wayman team beat the Rams in two straight tries. Members of the Wayman Ice Company team (below) were Bill Sager, Sam Trescott, Elmer Joiner, Lynn Joiner, "Tiny" DeBolt, Ray Amidon, Walter Kulow, John Hietanen, Andy Pastor, Alvin Norton, and Frank Wickert. Owner L. J. Wayman is pictured at left in the cap. George Spear, at center with his hands on his hips, served as a judge.

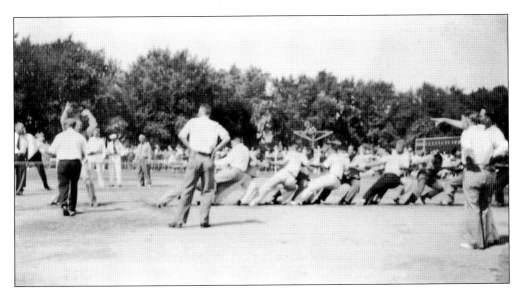

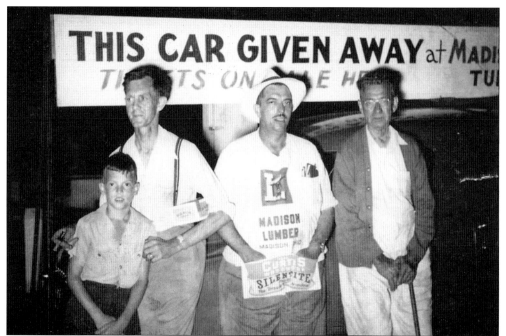

The Harvest Festival had evolved over the years to include a wide variety of entertainment. Harry Burnstein served as planner. He introduced exhibition boxing matches at an arena in the ballpark and brought in Golden Gloves fighters. There were footraces and potato sack races for children. A car raffle was a popular feature. Shown from left to right are Al Titman, Frank Blair, and Herschel Newby. The boy is unidentified.

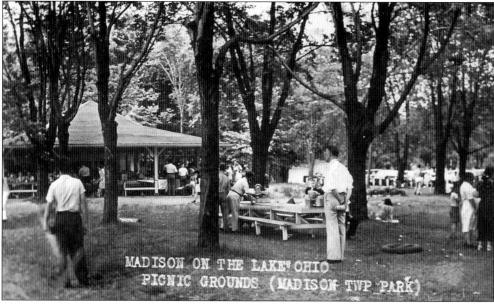

This view of a crowd enjoying the Madison Township Park picnic shelter was taken in the 1950s. As the site of some of Madison's earliest gatherings, the natural beauty of the park still provides a relaxing place for summer fun. In recent years, the park facility has received updates, including wave barriers for erosion abatement.

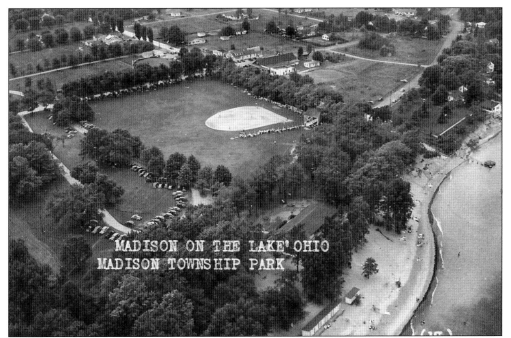

This aerial view of Madison Township Park shows the ball diamond, picnic pavilion, beach with changing rooms, and a boat dock. In the distance is the intersection of Hubbard and Lake Roads with its dance hall, restaurants, stores, and roller rink. Lake Erie's shore is a unique, natural gift that Madison still offers to its residents and visitors.

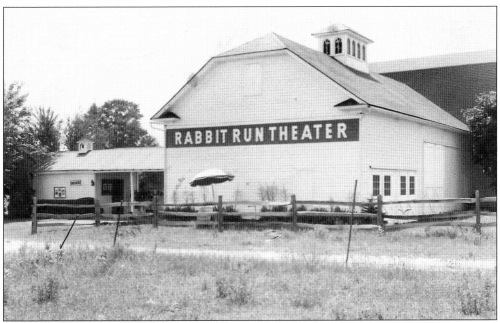

A barn that Frederick Foster built on his property at 5648 West Chapel Road in 1893 would eventually become a historic landmark. In 1918, Will and Marney Klump purchased the Foster farm. After returning from the U.S. army in 1946, Klump decided to follow a dream. He remodeled his barn into a theater and formed a summer stock theater, dubbing it Rabbit Run. (RRCAA.)

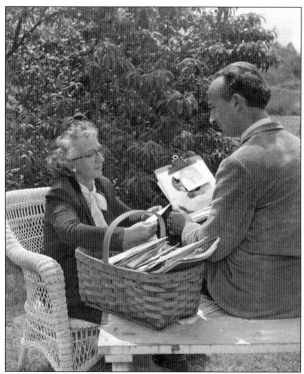

The Rabbit Run Theater became a success in its very first season in 1946. The 196-seat "straw-hat" theater was filled to capacity each week. The Klumps reviewed applications for actors and brought many beginning, but now famous, actors to their stage. This photograph of Marney and Will Klump was taken in 1955. (RRCAA.)

The Rabbit Run barn theater was named for the rabbits that ran throughout the farm. It opened the season in 1947 with the play *George Washington Slept Here*. The cast included in this scene are, from left to right, Robert Allman, local resident Dick Bates, theater owner Will Klump, and Marjorie Gundersen Springer. (RRCAA.)

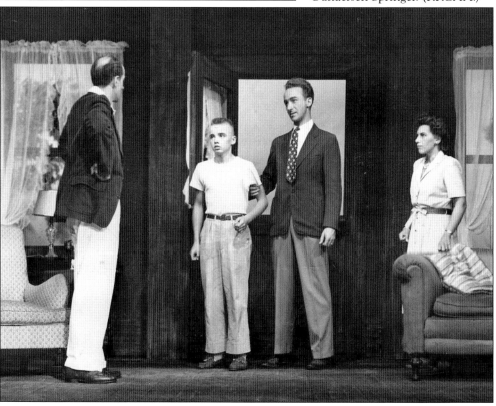

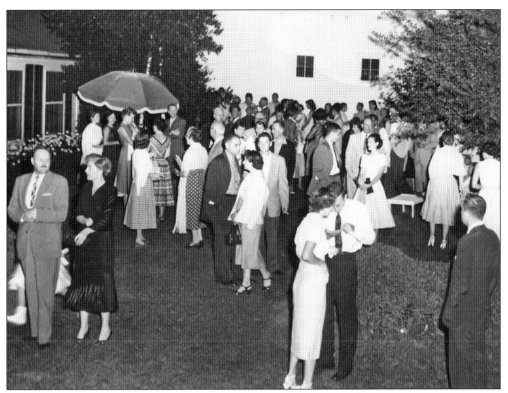

In 1955, a stage house was added to the barn theater, increasing the seating capacity to 300. Newspaper clippings dubbed it the "best equipped Straw Hat Theater in Ohio." This 1956 photograph shows intermission during a fund-raising performance at Rabbit Run. The Cleveland theater community had been invited to see what Rabbit Run offered. (RRCAA.)

From 1946 to the mid-1950s, the official photographer for Rabbit Run was Walter Bates. Here he captured Jim Backus (left) as Sheridan Whiteside in *The Man Who Came to Dinner* in 1953. Other famous actors who appeared at Rabbit Run included Hume Cronyn, Jessica Tandy, Dustin Hoffman, Sandy Dennis, Charles Grodin, Diana Hyland, and Marge Redmond. (RRCAA.)

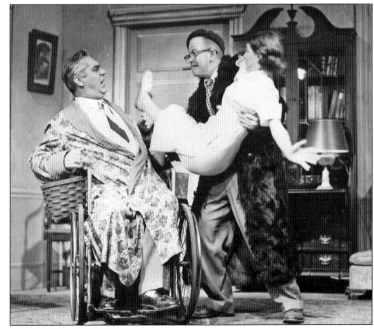

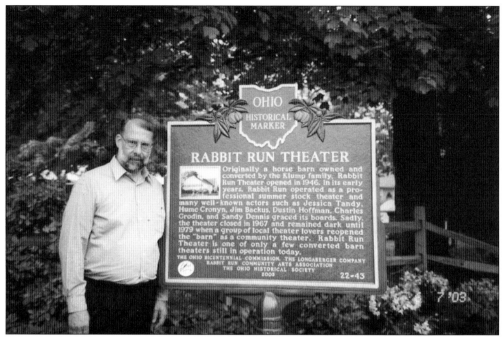

Rabbit Run closed in 1967, reopening in 1979 as Friends of Rabbit Run. In 2000, the community theater merged with Western Reserve Fine Arts to become the current Rabbit Run Community Arts Association. In 2001, Madison Township purchased the theater property to ensure its preservation. On June 7, 2003, an Ohio Historical Marker, shown here with association historian William Birk, was placed outside the Rabbit Run Theater. (RRCAA.)

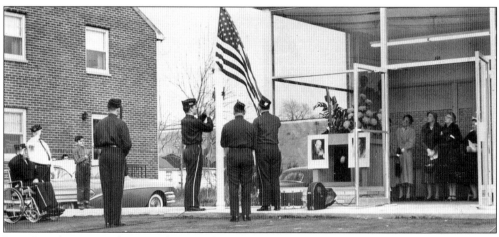

Pres. Dwight D. Eisenhower's photograph hangs on the window at the 1960 dedication of the new post office on Hubbard Road, south of North Ridge Road. North Madison was assigned zip code 44058. The building was vacated in 1975 when a larger facility was erected at 375 North Lake Street in Madison Village. Township and village postal services were consolidated, and the entire area was assigned the 44057 zip code.

Seven

LEARNING AND GATHERING

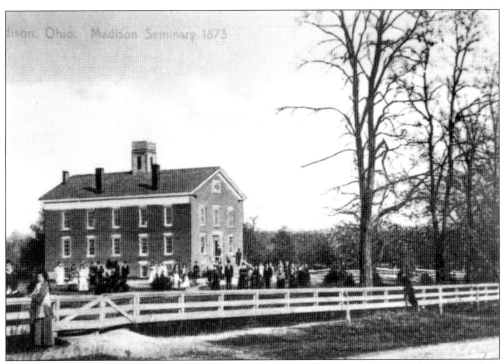

In 1847, the Madison Seminary was established at 6765 Middle Ridge Road in Madison Township. The seminary provided higher education to men and women of Lake County and beyond. This brick building was added to an original frame structure in 1859. The view in this photo postcard is dated 1873. The seminary closed as a school in July 1891, when it was purchased by the Ohio Women's Relief Corps.

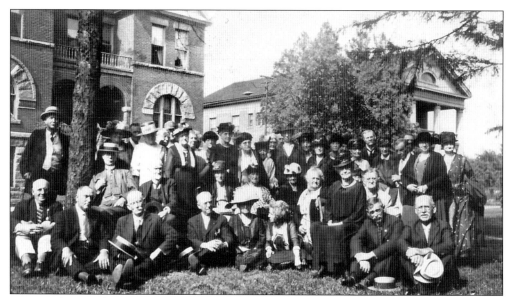

Many students graduating from the Madison Seminary went on to have distinguished careers. Some traveled to distant locations; others remained in Madison. Reunions were held starting in 1893 and continued at least until 1931, when the reunion register book lists 39 attendees. This undated photograph shows alumni posing in front of the seminary building on Middle Ridge Road.

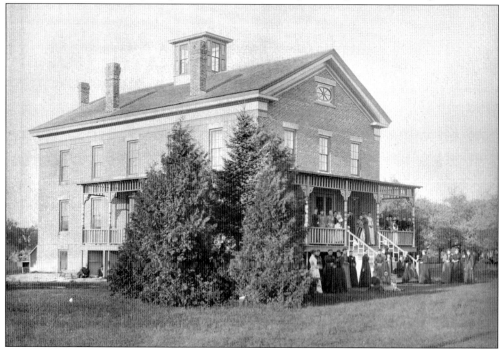

In 1888, the Women's Relief Corps determined that Civil War nurses and soldiers' mothers, wives, and sisters needed assistance and housing. A national search determined the Madison Seminary building in Madison was the best location. The building, 10 acres of land, and $1,000 cash were donated by the people of Madison and Geneva. In July 1891, the reconditioned seminary was dedicated as the new National Relief Corps Home.

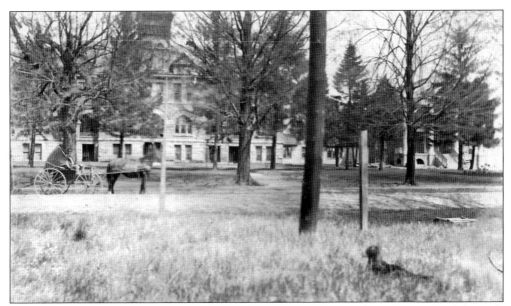

The original National Relief Corp Home was soon outgrown. A plan was suggested for each state to construct a building upon the home grounds. The State of Ohio took the first (and only) initiative and appropriated $25,000 for the construction of a "suitable cottage home for the indigent mothers and widows . . . of the late war." On November 10, 1892, the four-story Ohio Cottage was dedicated. This photograph is dated 1909.

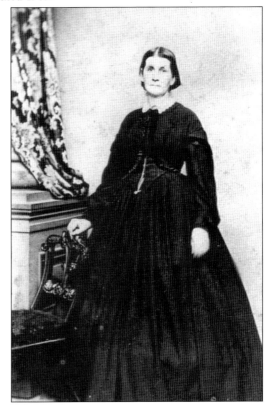

The National Relief Corps Home had many residents, but the most notorious was Elizabeth Stiles. Stiles was born Elizabeth Brown on August 21, 1816, in Ashtabula, Ohio. She was recruited by Pres. Abraham Lincoln and served as a spy and dispatch bearer for the Union during the Civil War. She became a resident at the National Relief Corps Home in 1895 and was buried in the adjacent cemetery in 1898.

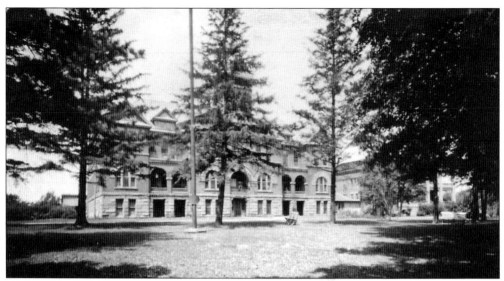

The Madison Home officially closed in 1962. Over the years, under the ownership of the State of Ohio, it served as a women's reformatory and housing for the developmentally disabled. In the 1970s, it housed the Madison Township administrative offices. In 1998, Lake County sold the building and surrounding land to Cass-Mill Nurseries, Inc. The Madison Home and Seminary buildings are listed on the National Register of Historic Places.

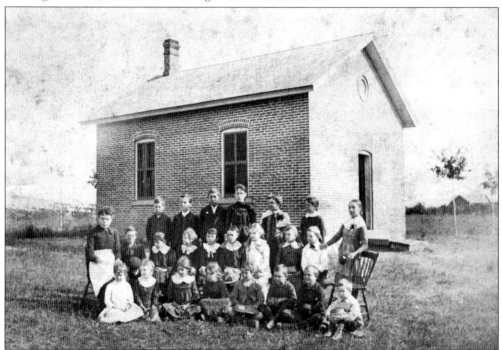

The first township schoolhouse was erected near Unionville in 1802. In 1815, the log cabin Block School House was built on the northwest corner of Madison Village Square. In 1853, the Madison Board of Education was organized, with schoolhouses throughout the township. This 1887 photograph shows the Pinetree School, which traditionally has been identified as the building at 5813 North Ridge Road. The teacher was Anna Burke.

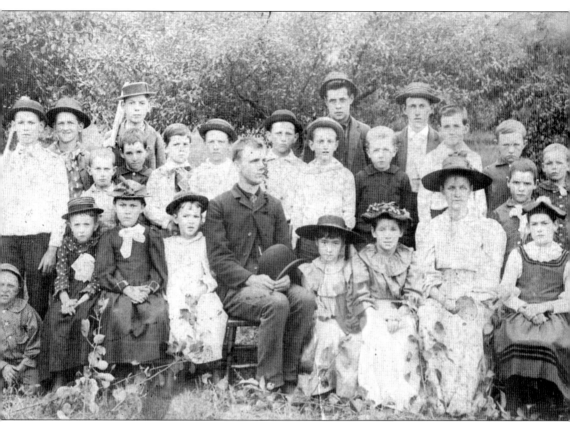

The students of the one-room Madison District 12 School posed for this photograph in 1892. The District 12 School was located near 6741 North Ridge Road where the board of education building is today. From left to right are (first row) John Dunsha, Eva Hill, Nell Brockway, Elsie Hall, Charles Chaffee, Ethel Hardy, Grace St. John, Florence Crocker, and Nell Corlett; (second row) Elmer Janes, John Hall, Orvia Hotchkiss, Guy St. John, Sherm Corlett, Frank Brockway, George Davet, Tom Hearn, Ed Davet, Parker Southwick, Paul Patchin, Frank Davet, Carl Hill, Carey Hearn, Archie Southwick, and Victor Chaffee. Teacher Charles Chaffee was the father of Victor, who was later a teacher and principal in Madison schools.

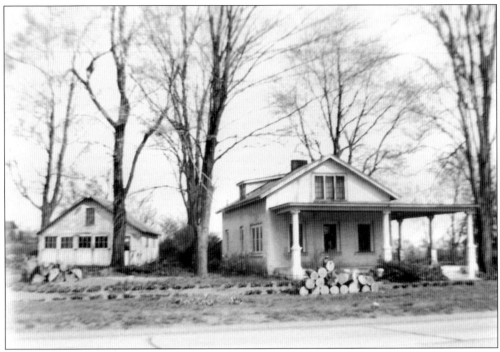

This photograph dated April 1955 shows the home of Dobler and Gertrude Vanderslice. The home at 5813 North Ridge Road had been converted from a schoolhouse to residential use. Many other schoolhouses across Madison were also purchased by individuals and remodeled. Others were eventually torn down. The small schoolhouses remained in use until about 1900, when Madison converted to a consolidated school system and began to build larger schools.

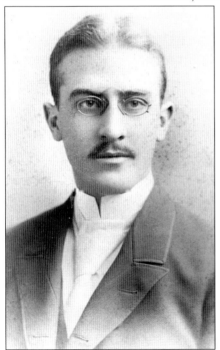

Homer Nash Kimball, son of Lemuel Hastings Kimball, graduated from Oberlin College in 1890. His major was listed as "philosophical." Returning to Madison, he joined the family banking business and became a leader in modernizing public education. He was superintendent of Madison Schools, served on the Board of School Examiners, and was elected to the Ohio Legislature. Homer Nash Kimball Elementary School on River Street was named after him.

John Roswell Adams is credited with the idea to centralize Madison Township schools. Born in Leroy, Ohio, in 1854, he was educated at the Painesville Academy and Mount Union College. Adams moved to Unionville in 1878. He taught at Unionville School for 29 consecutive years. Beginning in 1895, Adams served as the superintendent of Madison Township Schools. In 1904, he followed Homer Nash Kimball on the Board of School Examiners.

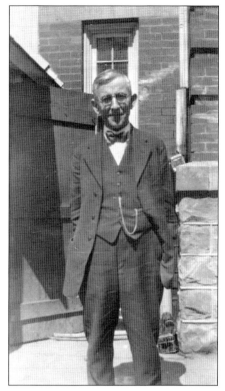

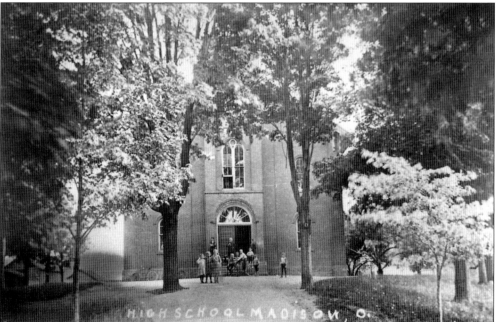

In 1867, a large school was constructed on Main Street, on the hill just west of River Street in the village. The school was a model for its time. All grades attended the school until it was replaced by newer buildings. The building was closed permanently in 1927. The walk leading to the old building became the driveway for the Homer Nash Kimball Elementary north addition.

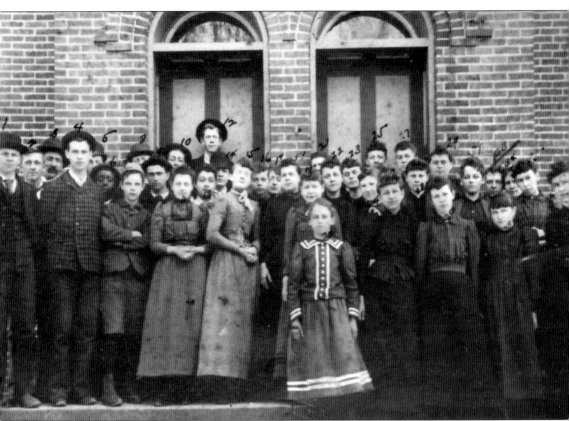

The class of 1893–1894 gathered outside the original Madison High School for a portrait. Pictured are (1) John Safford, (2) Glenn Cady, (3) Prof. Foote, (4) Norman Bliss, (5) Wilbur Parks (?), (6) G. Brown (?), (7) Will Couch, (8) Brewster Safford, (9) Bert Blakely, (10) Bert Holbrook, (11) Minnie Adams, (12) Sherman Parks, (13) Clara Halstead, (14) Carl Kimball, (15) Cora Maud Turney, (16) Emma Donahue, (17) Bessie May Bliss, (18) Jennie Upton, (19) Carrie Ludick, (20) Mabel Toop, (21) unidentified, (22) Mamie Woodworth, (23) Nellie Skinner, (24) Lucy Whipple, (25) Anna Hearn, (26) Alice Murphy, (27) Rachel Smead, (28) Alma Follett, (29) Marion Skinner, (30) Nellie Quirk, (31) Winnie Snell, (32) Grace Heartwell, (33) Nell Sunderland Harper, (34) Gladys Tuttle, (35) Kate Collister, and (36) Alwilda Stearns.

Be Sure to Come!

THE SIXTH ANNUAL BANQUET

Of the Alumni of Madison High School will be held

On Wednesday Evening, June 14th, 1899,

at the Residence of Dr. and Mrs. J. H. Quayle.

●●● *The Stranahan Bros. Catering Co., of Cleveland, will Serve the Supper.* ●●●
A Mandolin Club will Furnish Music.

Please notify the Secretary not later than Monday, June 12, if you expect to attend. It is hoped that a very large number of our members will be present. Annual dues seventy-five cents.

BESSIE M. BLISS, Secretary.

Madison, Ohio, May 25th, 1899.

High school classes gathered for annual banquets starting in 1893. This invitation was for the sixth annual banquet, held on July 14, 1899. It was held at the residence of Dr. Charles H. and Nellie Quayle, with catering by the Stranahan Brothers Catering Company of Cleveland. Music was provided by a mandolin club. The invitation was mailed out by class secretary Bessie M. Bliss and is dated May 25, 1899.

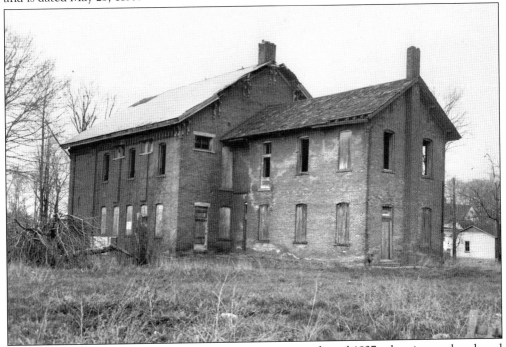

The village school at Main Street near River Street was used until 1927, when it was abandoned and fell into decay. This view of the back of the old school was taken in 1957 prior to its demolition. The cleared property was used to construct an addition to Homer Nash Kimball Elementary School.

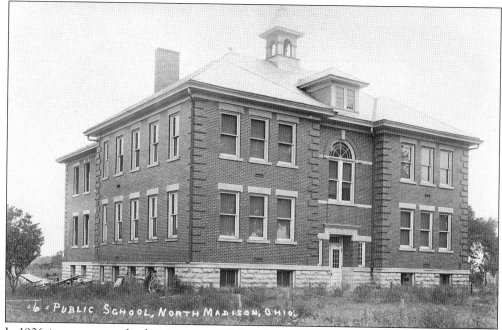

In 1906, in response to the decision to consolidate the small schoolhouses, this large building was constructed on the site of the one-room school at 6741 North Ridge Road. It was named North Madison School. The building served both primary and high school students. This photograph was taken shortly after the building's completion.

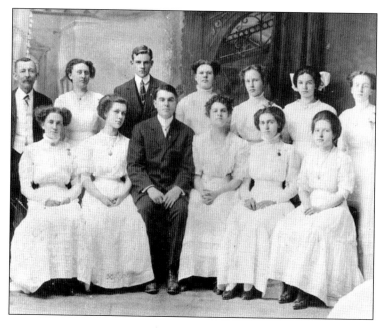

The first North Madison School graduating class in 1910 gathered for their portrait. From left to right are (first row) Cynthia Brew Sprague, Adelaide Hess Bowen, Fred Brower, Ruth Blanchard Pierce, Eva Brown Whipple, and Beatrice Shaw Court; (second row) Prof. John Roswell Adams, Mary Shepard Bobel, James Clark, Ruth Busse, Julia Noyes Lamb, Flora Harris Rand, and Cora Vesey Forke.

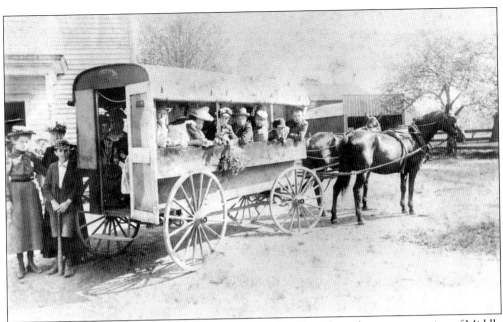

Leon Brotzman owned and drove this horse-drawn school bus along the eastern portion of Middle Ridge Road, delivering students to North Madison School. This photograph was taken in 1902 outside the original wood North Madison schoolhouse. Some of the students shown are Roland Standish, Ned Miller, Nelson Collister, Ralph Stimpert, Ray Miller, Pearl Crandall, Alice Huber, Grace Olds, and Sam Hathaway. The horses were Comet and Francie.

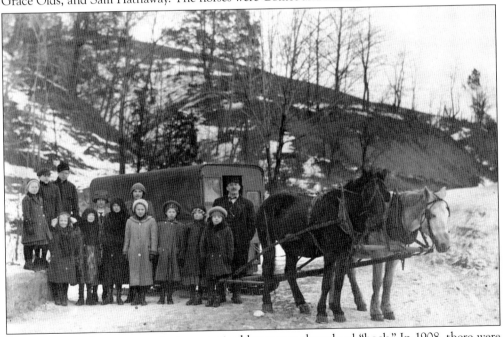

The transportation system prior to motorized buses was the school "hack." In 1908, there were 18 hack routes in Madison Township serving the many small schoolhouses. This horse-drawn wagon was fitted with runners in the winter. Here a group of students poses with its driver in South Madison near the Grand River around 1915.

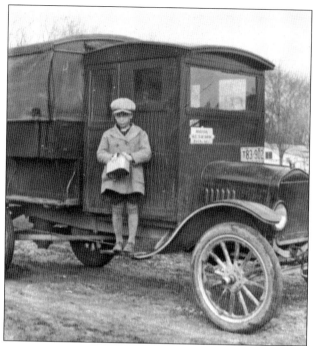

In 1926, a motorized school bus picked up students like little Ted Aldrich near his home on Chapel Road. Harley Smith, the driver, drove the school bus all eight years Aldrich attended North Madison School. The bus windows had canvas curtains that rolled up, and a sign advertising the Madison Glee Club shows in the front window.

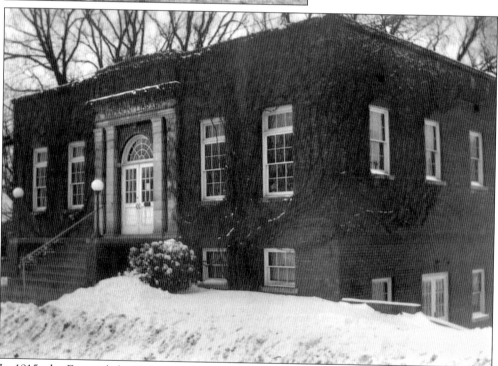

In 1915, the Fortnightly Club of Madison, a literary group, formed the Madison Village and Township Free Library Association. Members petitioned for a grant to build a public library under the Carnegie Library Program. The land at 126 West Main Street in Madison Village, the former site of the Madison Steam Mills, was donated by the Quayle family. The building was constructed for $10,000 by C. H. Stocking, Contractors.

The Madison Public Library opened on April 26, 1919. The first librarian was Agnes Martin. This 1962 photograph shows librarian Hesper Kellogg on the steps, while Gil McLean holds the ladder for Herbert Swaby as he installs a new sign. The library operated at this site until a new facility was erected on Middle Ridge Road in 1974. This building then became the Madison Village Hall and police headquarters.

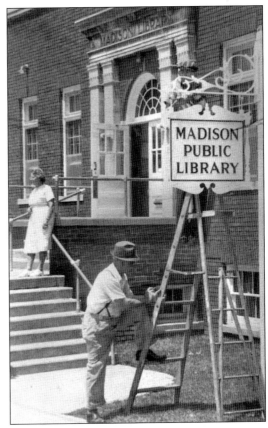

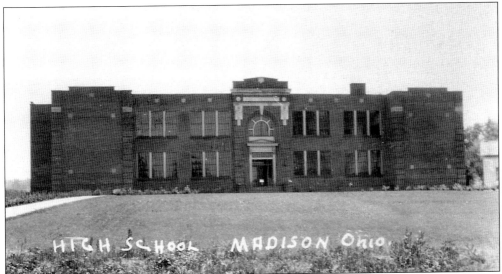

In 1921, the Memorial High School building at 92 East Main Street opened. A consolidated high school for all of Madison was now possible. High school students from both the Madison Village School and North Madison School had their own building. Memorial High School was named in honor of Madison's servicemen. A bell installed on the high school lawn was from the old Main Street village school.

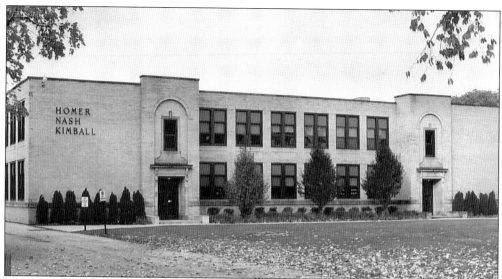

School buildings continued to be constructed across the Madison School District. In 1923, South Madison Elementary was built on Ross Road. In 1926, Homer Nash Kimball Elementary School, shown here, was built on River Street. In 1958, Red Bird Elementary was built on Red Bird Road in North Madison. Madison gained a separate junior high school in 1962 with the construction of a building at 1941 Red Bird Road.

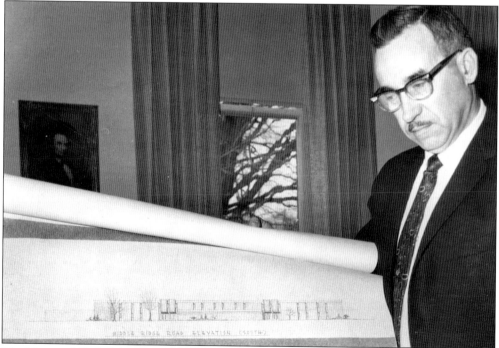

The Memorial High School served the community well until overcrowding and an aging building brought the need for a more modern facility. In this photograph dated March 13, 1969, Al J. Barr, superintendent of schools, holds the plans for a new high school building to be constructed on Middle Ridge Road. A ground-breaking ceremony for the new Madison High School at Middle Ridge and Burns Roads was held on Sunday, August 10, 1969.

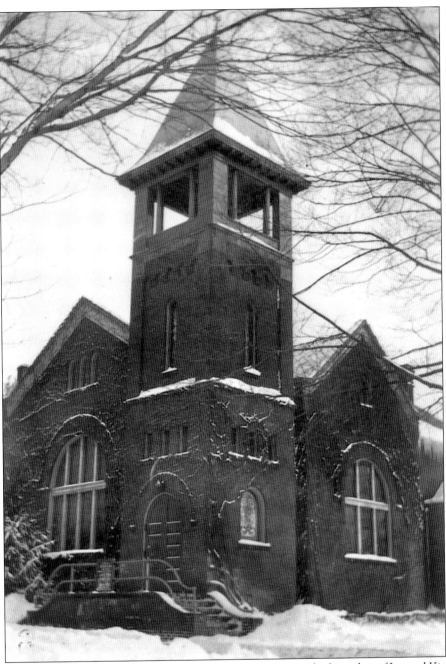

The Congregational church in Madison was organized in 1814 at the log cabin of Lemuel Kimball, at 467 West Main Street. Services later moved to the Block School House, located on the village square. In 1819, services moved to the townhouse at the northwest corner of Hubbard and Middle Ridge Roads. In 1828, the Congregationalists contributed to build a frame town hall facing the village square to use as a community church. It was the beginning of Township Hall. In 1842, the congregation built a frame church on the site of the present building at 71 Park Street. The Central Congregational Church building was later enlarged and faced with brick, as shown in this 1946 photograph.

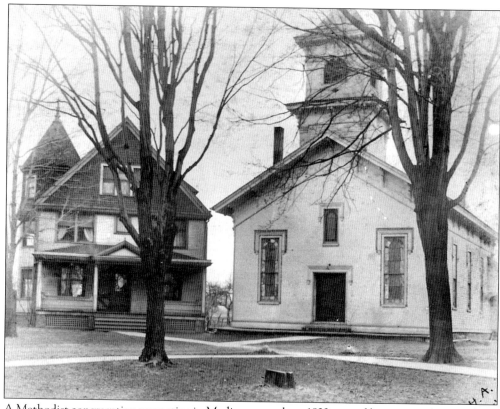

A Methodist congregation was active in Madison as early as 1822, served by circuit-rider preachers. The Park United Methodist Church building at 31 Park Street was constructed in 1865. In 1946, an organ was installed in memory of Will Adlard, who served as superintendent of the Sunday school for 33 years. The parsonage next door was moved to Saxton Street in the 1960s. This photograph was taken in 1908.

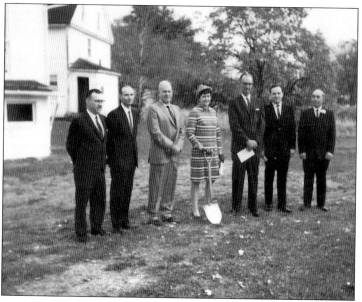

In 1968, the Park United Methodist Church held a ceremonial ground-breaking for their new Wesley Building. The new space would accommodate Sunday school classes and church activities. The ground-breaking committee members are, from left to right, Al Barr, Rev. Richard Haney, Dr. Donald Klingbeil, Elizabeth Behm, architects Walter Ronk and Herk Visnapuu, and Perry Quayle.

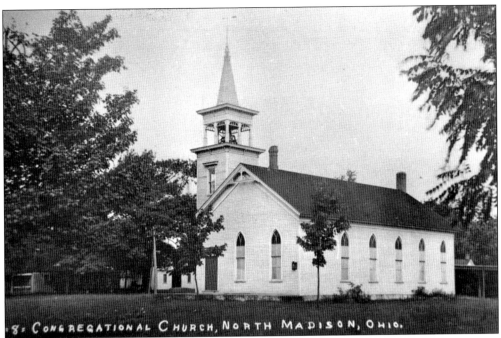

8: CONGREGATIONAL CHURCH, NORTH MADISON, OHIO.

In 1835, the First Congregational Church and Society of North Madison built the Bell Meeting House at the northeast corner of North Ridge and Hubbard Roads. In 1889, the church burned to the ground. It was rebuilt and dedicated in 1891, as seen here. In 1965, it was sold by the Bible Baptist Church. The church was moved north to 2525 Hubbard Road, and the corner became a gas station.

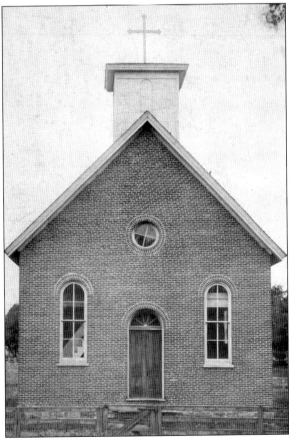

The first Madison Catholic Mass was celebrated by Rev. John Tracy of Ashtabula in 1863 at the home of Cornelius Roark at 150 Safford Street. In 1868, Reverend Tracy organized contributions to build a church, which was built the same year. The church was located at 15 Lake Street in Madison Village and finally dedicated on July 27, 1884. The parish was named Church of the Immaculate Conception.

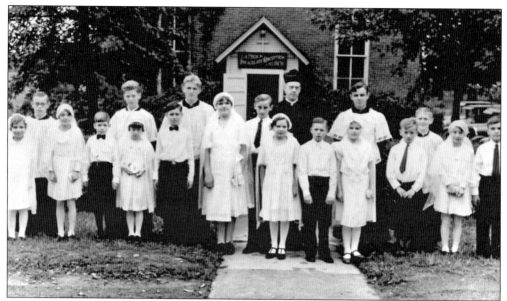

From 1869 until 1934, the Madison Immaculate Conception Church remained a monthly mission and was attached to the parish of Painesville. In August 1934, Immaculate Conception was assigned its first resident pastor, the Reverend Ludwig Joseph Virant. Here Father Virant poses with a First Communion class in front of the old church. In 1953, the Immaculate Conception Church community moved to a new building at 2846 Hubbard Road.

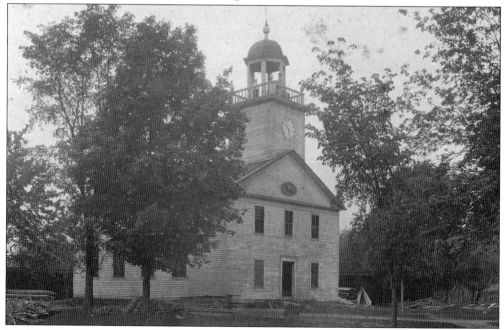

Madison Baptists first met in 1811 at the home of Asa Turney. In 1831, the First Baptist Church of Madison was officially organized with 16 members. Azariah Hanks was the pastor. This church at the northeast corner of Middle Ridge and Hubbard Roads was dedicated in 1842. William H. Genung painted the clock tower hands, frozen at 10:29, to remind members of the correct time to be seated for services.

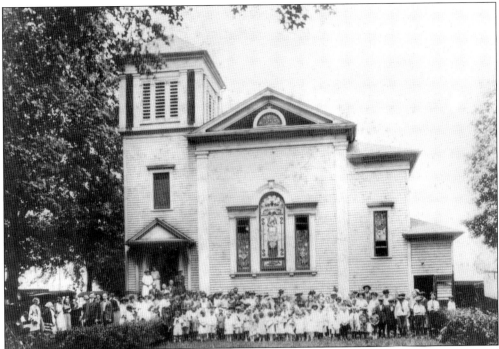

The First Baptist Church of Madison at Middle Ridge and Hubbard Roads eventually needed more space for services and Sunday school classes. The old church was rebuilt in 1900 and enlarged again in 1922 to give it the appearance shown here. Another major expansion in 1959 modernized the structure.

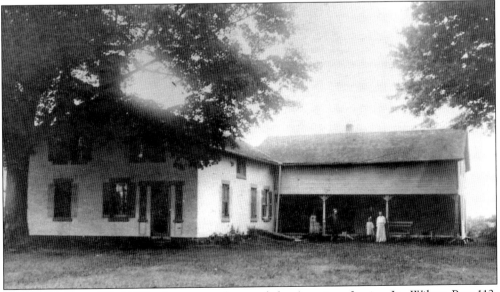

In 1923, Madison World War I veterans chartered the American Legion Jay Wilson Post 112. Under the slogan "In peace as in war we serve," the group met at Township Hall on the village square. In the 1960s, they purchased property for a headquarters at 6671 Middle Ridge Road just west of the Lake Street intersection. The headquarters is shown as it appeared around 1900 when it was the Onderdunk homestead.

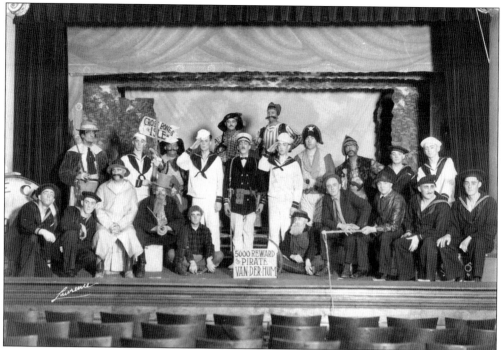

Music was especially important in the development of Madison. As early as 1815, Joseph Talcott conducted a singing group at the Block School House. In 1906, the Madison Glee Club was formed. Its activities helped fund auditoriums in Memorial High School and the junior high. Costumed performances were a highlight of the Madison Glee Club. Seen above in 1924, they had a nautical theme. Shown below, the 1924 Madison Glee Club members are, from left to right, (first row) Wendell Williams, Leo Long, Fred Leyde, Carl Kimball, Don Wheeler, Robert Bates, and Stanley Bates; (second row) Will Adlard, Carl Weldy, Alfred Titman, Clarence Brown, Abel Kimball, Karl Keiffer, and Carroll Van Dyke; (third row) Delos Bates, Edward Rose, Howard Pearce, R. O. Bibschman, Charles Liukart, and Mark Miricle; (fourth row) Glenn Haskins, Harry Titman, Fred Bates, Sam Trescott, Harlan Metcalf, John Henning, and Carl Lawson.

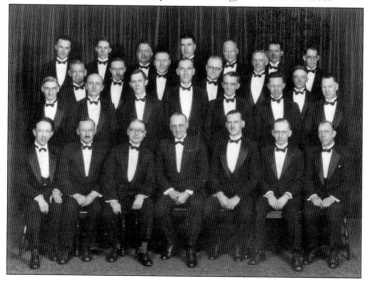

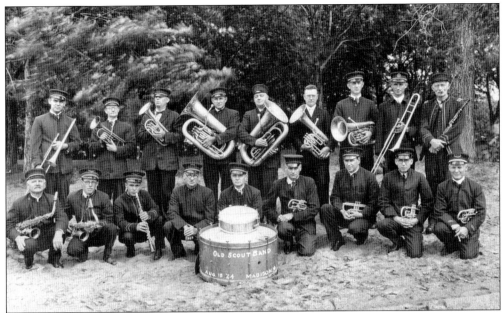

Records of instrumental music in Madison go back to 1801, when John Walworth hosted a Fourth of July celebration featuring a fife and drum band. Madison's first formal instrumental band was formed in 1819. In the early 1900s, the Madison Concordia Band was formed but suspended during World War I. Bandmaster Jacob Schworm formed the Old Scout Band, shown here in 1924. Schworm is standing at the back right.

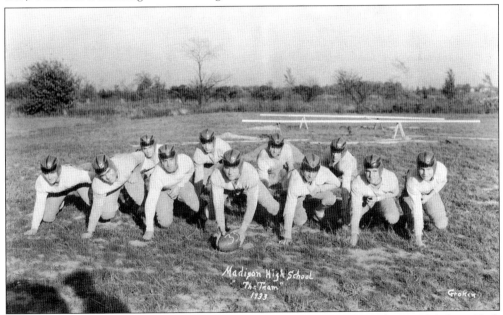

Community and school sports are another way Madison citizens gather. The 1933 Madison High School football team, led by coach Frank J. Tarr, was the largest team to date. From left to right are (first row) Russell Whipple, Hudson Whipple, Edward Gabor, Edward Gola, Lowell Green, Walter Garrett, and Dallas Candy; (second row) Lynn Miller, team captain Walter Bates, Robert Beall, and Mert Brewster. (AG.)

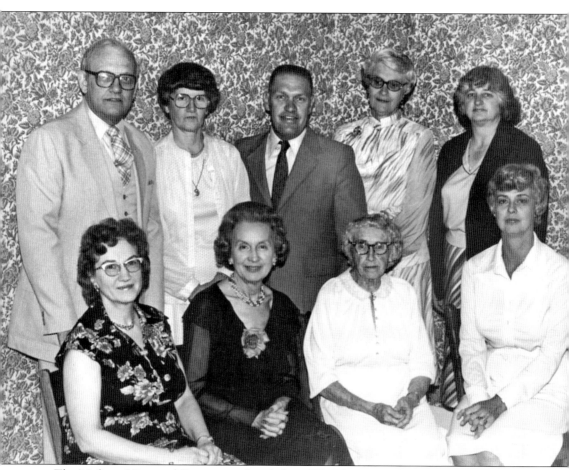

The Madison Historical Society was founded in 1978. The nonprofit organization's mission is to collect, preserve, display, and make accessible to the public historical information about Madison Village and Madison Township and their citizens. The first Madison Historical Society board, shown here from left to right, consisted of (first row) secretary Geraldine Rhodes, president Louanna Billington, Catherine B. Rose, and vice president Donna Keyse; (second row) James Waterman, Rosemary Wayman, Richard Hart, treasurer Louise Sedgely, and Lois Stanton. This group and 103 charter members raised public awareness of the rich historical fabric of Madison and the need to preserve its stories and valuable artifacts. Thousands of volunteer hours have resulted in a vast collection of photographs, information, and significant museum-quality items from Madison's past. Efforts continue to keep this material safe and available to the public. In 2010, the Madison Historical Society celebrates 32 years of preserving Madison's history.

INDEX

www.arcadiapublishing.com

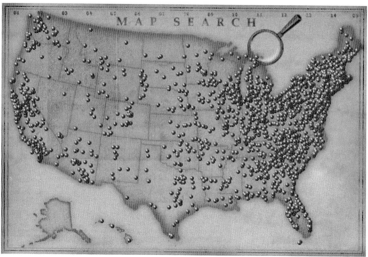

Discover books about the town where you grew up, the cities where your friends and families live, the town where your parents met, or even that retirement spot you've been dreaming about. Our Web site provides history lovers with exclusive deals, advanced notification about new titles, e-mail alerts of author events, and much more.

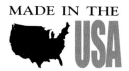

MADE IN THE
USA

Arcadia Publishing, the leading local history publisher in the United States, is committed to making history accessible and meaningful through publishing books that celebrate and preserve the heritage of America's people and places. Consistent with our mission to preserve history on a local level, this book was printed in South Carolina on American-made paper and manufactured entirely in the United States.

This book carries the accredited Forest Stewardship Council (FSC) label and is printed on 100 percent FSC-certified paper. Products carrying the FSC label are independently certified to assure consumers that they come from forests that are managed to meet the social, economic, and ecological needs of present and future generations.

FSC
Mixed Sources
Product group from well-managed
forests and other controlled sources

Cert no. SW-COC-001530
www.fsc.org
© 1996 Forest Stewardship Council

Find Your Place in History.